HOW METEORS
HIT THE GROUND 2
Detailed Accident
Statistics Added

Geoffrey Higges

ISBN-10: 1499275617
ISBN-13: 978-1499275612

DEDICATION

To the memory of good friends on 42 Pilots Course,
616 Squadron and 501 Squadron, 1949 to 1957.

CONTENTS

Acknowledgements   7

1. How I Nearly Hit the Ground   9

2. The Story Starts with Frank Whittle   16

3. Development of the Gloster Meteor   19

4. The Highs and Lows of Pilot Training   24

5. How to Become a Jet Pilot   32

6. How to Become a Fighter Pilot   38

7. Life on a Fighter Squadron   42

8. Gloster Meteor Characteristics   49

9. More Near Death Experiences   56

10. A Page of Statistics   66

Appendix 1: Extracts from Pilot's Notes   68
        for Meteor 8 – 1955
Appendix 2: Detailed Crash Statistics   93
        1945 to 1957
Appendix 3: Abbreviations   132

References   134

ACKNOWLEDGEMENTS

To my wife Carole-Anne Fooks for editing and support.

To J. J. Halley for his book of aircraft accident statistics "Broken Wings" published by Air-Britain (Historians) Limited.

1. How I Nearly Hit the Ground

I checked inside the cockpit of the Gloster Meteor 8 single-seat fighter aircraft to make sure that the undercarriage selector lever was fully down, and that the control locks were removed. Then I checked that the hydraulic pressure was at least 800 pounds per square inch, that the parking brake was on, that the brake pressure was at least 200 pounds per square inch, and that there was sufficient oxygen. I climbed out of the cockpit and carried out the usual cursory walk around the aircraft, looking first to make sure that the cover was removed from the pitot head which fed the aircraft's forward speed to the cockpit instrument panel. Then I checked for anything else out of place such as any signs of damage or loose inspection panels. I confirmed with the ground crew that the external battery was plugged in and switched on, ready to start the engines.

I climbed back into the cockpit, fixed my safety harness, and with a glance around the cockpit half checked the fifty or so items on the pre-start check list. I pressed the starter button of the port engine for two seconds, and opened the left high pressure fuel cock half way. As the engine rpm approached idling speed of about 3,000 rpm the high pressure cock was gently opened fully. Then the starboard engine was started.

Gloster Meteor 8 of 616 South Yorkshire Squadron,
RAF Finningley, 1953

It was a Saturday morning in 1953 at Royal Air Force Finningley, near Doncaster in South Yorkshire in England, and although the sun was not shining it was not a dull day. I taxied the Meteor 8 of 616 Squadron of the Royal Auxiliary Air Force to the takeoff point. In fact the sky was a light haze of milky cloud, impossible to tell from the ground at what level the cloud started, nor how high it reached.

Generally in squadron exercises we would fly in operational formations of two or four or more, but today I was carrying out a lone exercise to test the local Approach and Landing radar systems by climbing to 20,000 feet, with the intention of calling Ground Control to ask them to direct me back to Finningley for an approach using the Instrument Landing System.

I aligned the Meteor 8 for takeoff, applied the brakes, and checked that they held the aircraft stationary while the throttles were opened to give 11,000 rpm on each engine. Releasing the brakes, the throttles were opened fully and a quick check made of the engines' speed – 14,550 rpm, jet pipe temperatures below 680 degrees Celsius, and fire warning lights out. The Meteor 8 accelerated rapidly and the nose wheel was eased off the ground at 70 knots, making sure not to hit the tail on the ground by raising the nose wheel too high. At 130 knots the Meteor flies itself off the ground. The undercarriage was retracted - before 175 knots, the flaps raised, and the climb began at 300 knots indicated airspeed with full power still set.

Soon after takeoff I entered the wispy cloud and found myself in a white world with no horizon, having to rely entirely on the rudimentary instruments in the cockpit of the Meteor 8. Of course I was well trained and experienced in instrument flying, so theoretically that posed no threat. As it turned out the cloud reached all the way up to 20,000 feet, providing an ideal opportunity to test the Ground Control radar for my approach and landing back at Finningley.

I now started turning casually back 180 degrees while expecting to temporarily level off at 20,000 feet, preparatory to calling Ground Control for the start of the exercise. However, it seems that for a few seconds (in spite of my experience) I was not concentrating well enough on the crucial instruments which give attitude, altitude and speed, in a situation where there was no horizon to see – just whiteness all around. So when proper concentration was resumed I was surprised to find I had turned more than expected, was increasing speed, and disturbingly I had lost several hundred feet in the turn. All of which didn't worry me too much while I carried out what I thought were normal corrective procedures.

But my "normal corrective actions" had no effect, and I soon found myself nearing 18,000 feet with my speed having increased from 0.63 Mach Number at the top of the climb to 0.70 plus.

Compared to modern aircraft,
the Meteor cockpit design was very crude.

Upper row: Mach no., airspeed, artificial horizon, vertical speed (climb/descent rate), port engine rpm.
Second row: undercarriage lights (up/down), altimeter, compass, slip/skid (yawmeter), engine exhaust temperatures

By now I was getting rather worried. Remember there was nothing to see outside the aeroplane other than the all-pervading whiteness. I was all alone in my tiny cockpit with an instrument panel a few inches from my face with my trustworthy instruments beginning to look entirely untrustworthy! After a few more seconds of trying desperately to correct the situation by manoeuvring the controls in what I was sure was the right action, the control column was now becoming more and more rigid and difficult to move. It was now time to panic!

That is when it flashed through my mind: "This is how so many pilots have lost their lives in Meteors, by diving inexplicably out of cloud into the ground!" So I decided to bale out and grabbed the handle which when pulled would set off the ejector seat rockets. Would I survive baling out at such a high speed? On second thoughts I didn't think so (and there are many examples which suggest I was correct in this assumption). So I took a very deep breath and once more fiercely concentrated on the instruments which I had always believed in throughout my previous experience. Check: speed – almost Mach 0.8, nearing the limit of the Meteor, altimeter – going down rapidly through 15,000 feet, confirmed by the vertical speed indicator; artificial horizon – at first sight it seemed to be at such a crazy angle that it might not have been working at all, but finally (after about one second or less), I could see that it did show a steep bank to the left and a steep nose down attitude. Lastly I checked the slip and skid indicator – this shows whether the aircraft is yawing left or right, which it could do if the aircraft was in a stalled spin (usually slow speed), but it was pretty well dead centre.

Strangely everything seemed to be quite plain. I was in a quite recognisable "high speed spiral dive". In other words I was banking and turning to the left, and heading downwards at 800 kilometres per hour. So the corrective procedure seemed to be obvious – what I had been trying to do all the time - moving the control column to the right to straighten up, and moving it back to pull out of the dive. (Normally the movements that are required to control an aircraft are quite small with relatively moderate force, but now the control column seemed to be rock solid.)

One last try. With both hands on the control column and bracing myself as much as I could against the side of the seat and the cockpit, I used all my strength to push the control column to the right to counteract the spiralling left, aided by my right foot pushing as hard as possible on the right rudder. I was amazed and relieved when finally the Artificial Horizon showed that I had straightened the aircraft - but I was still diving, now straight ahead, at maximum speed.

I knew that the Meteor was susceptible to breaking up if it was pulled out of a dive too sharply, so I now had the dilemma of requiring all my strength to pull back on the column smoothly! Imagine the relief when a few seconds later I found the aircraft heading upwards through 9,000 feet and losing speed rapidly, which I was soon able to correct and level out. So I didn't have to bale out, nor fly into the ground, and I was able to continue with the planned exercise.

It is with this unforgettable experience in mind that 50 years later, after seeing many similar incidents revealed in the book "Broken Wings" by James J. Halley M.B.E., that I am prompted to jot down this experience, together with some others. For example Halley records that in 1952 a Meteor was written off 3 times every week on average, and a Meteor pilot was killed every 4 days, over a quarter of these deaths being due to a Meteor diving inexplicably into the ground on a cloudy day.

During my career flying Meteors between May 1951 and March 1957, over 50 Meteor pilots were killed in similar episodes, usually described officially in the records as "Unexplained dive into the ground out of cloud".

2. The Story Starts with Frank Whittle

Air Commodore Sir Frank Whittle
OM, KBE, CB, FRS, Hon FRAeS (1907–1996)

Frank Whittle is regarded as the father of aircraft gas turbine propulsion, his ideas coming several years prior to those of Germany's Dr. Hans von Ohain.

In 1923 he was accepted as an apprentice on his third attempt to join the Royal Air Force in England, eventually qualifying as a pilot in 1928, and later becoming a flying instructor at Wittering, where I did the ground training at the beginning of my pilot's course. During this period Frank Whittle wrote a thesis arguing for gas turbines or rockets to be needed for high flying aircraft, and in 1930 he patented a gas turbine design.

Whittle was continually pestering the British Air Ministry for funds to assist his research, but to no avail, so that in 1935 his patent lapsed because he could not afford the 5 pound fee. However just one year later Whittle was able to convince Investment Bankers O.T.Falk & Partners that *"The engine of the future must produce 2,000 hp with one moving part: a spinning turbine and compressor"*, so that with their backing he was able to form Power Jets Limited, and continue developing a gas turbine engine.

A replica of the Gloster E28/39, the first British jet aircraft

The Whittle/Power Jets gas turbine engine used in the
E28/39. It had a double-sided centrifugal compressor
and reverse flow combustion chambers.

Finally, in September 1939, the Air Ministry issued a
specification to Gloster for an aircraft to test one of Frank
Whittle's turbojet designs in flight. The E28/39 name comes
from the aircraft having been built to the 28th
"Experimental" specification issued by the Air Ministry in
1939. Gloster's chief designer George Carter worked closely
with Whittle, and designed a small low-wing aircraft of
conventional configuration. The jet intake was in the nose,
and the tail-fin and elevators were mounted above the jet-
pipe.

But it was not until nearly 2 years later on 15 May 1941, well
into the war with Germany, that the Gloster E28/39 first got
airborne powered by a Whittle engine. Gloster's Chief Test
Pilot, Flight Lieutenant Gerry Sayer flew the aircraft under
jet power for the first time from RAF Cranwell, near
Sleaford in Lincolnshire, in a flight lasting 17 minutes. In the
meantime, the German Heinkel He 178 designed by von
Ohain, had already taken to the air.

3. Development of the Gloster Meteor

In 1940 George Carter, the chief designer of the Gloster Aircraft Company in England, presented proposals for a twin-engine jet fighter. 3 years later, the first prototype Gloster Meteor jet fighter flies from RAF Cranwell, this time powered by two de Havilland Halford H.1 engines (which the same year were used to power the first De Havilland Vampire jet fighter).

The Gloster Meteor F1/F3 jet fighter, used by
RAF 616 Squadron in the latter stages of WW2

One year later in 1944, the Gloster Meteor F1 was rolling off the production lines, with Rolls Royce Derwent engines, which were the result of continuing development of the E28/39 Whittle engine by Power Jets, the Rover Car Company, and of course Rolls Royce.

The Rolls Royce Derwent engine which powered
the Gloster Meteor F1/F3

In 1944 RAF 616 Squadron received their first Meteor F1s, which soon after were replaced by F3s. 14 kills of German Flying Bomb V1's were claimed that year by the Meteors.

Wind tunnel and flight tests demonstrated that the original short nacelles of the F1 contributed heavily to compressibility buffeting at high speed, but longer nacelles in the F3 (and all later Meteors) not only cured some of the compressibility problems but added 120 km/h (75 mph) to its speed at altitude.

The first Gloster Meteor F4 prototype flew on 17 May 1945, later creating a world speed record of 616 mph (975 kph). It went into production in 1946, and soon there were 16 RAF squadrons equipped with Meteor 4s. From 1946 to 1948 over 600 Meteor F4 with Rolls Royce Derwent 5 engines were produced, including exports to Argentina (50), Belgium (48), Denmark (20), Egypt (12), and the Netherlands (38).

Meteor 4s of 203 Advanced Flying School,
RAF Carnaby, Yorkshire 1951

The Meteor 7 two-seat trainer,
developed from the Meteor 4 in 1949

The final versions of the single seat fighter were the Gloster Meteors 8 and 9. The Meteor 8 first flew on 12 October 1948, with Rolls Royce Derwent 8 jet engines. It featured a fuselage stretch of 76 cm, intended to shift the aircraft's centre of gravity, and drastically reduce the need for the 450kg of nose ballast in the previous versions of the Meteor. Other modifications included an extra fuselage fuel tank, structural strengthening and a Martin Baker ejection seat, and a "blown" teardrop cockpit canopy that provided improved pilot visibility.

Initially it was found that when ammunition was expended, the aircraft became tail-heavy and unstable due to the weight of fuel retained in fuselage tanks no longer being balanced by the ammunition. This was solved by a new tail with taller straighter edges, which also improved general stability, giving the later Meteor 8s their distinctive appearance compared to the rounded tail of the F4s and earlier marks.

Over 3000 Meteor 8s were produced with more than 10 variants, such as night fighters and photo-reconnaissance aircraft, and it was exported to 17 countries. In 1950-53 Meteor 8s were used by the Royal Australian Air Force Squadron 77 in the Korean War; initially in air-to-air combat (finding it difficult against the MIG), then more successfully in ground attack.

Brief Specifications of the Gloster Meteor 8

Engines: Two Rolls Royce Derwent 8, each 3600lb force (1636 kg f, 16kN); single stage, centrifugal flow turbojets

Fuselage Fuel Tanks Capacity: 325 Imperial Gallons Main Tank, 95 gallons extra Front Tank

Drop Tanks: Ventral Tank 175 Gallons, Wing Tanks 100 imp gall. each

Wingspan: 37' 2" (11.30 m);

Length: 44' 7" (13.59 m)

Wing Area: 350 square feet (32.51 sq. metres); Height: 13' 10" (4.22 m)

Weights: Empty 10,626 lb (4,820 kg); Maximum Take-off Weight: 19,100 lb (8,664 kg)

Armament: 4 x 20mm cannon, 2 x 1000lb bombs, or 8 x 60 lb air to ground rockets

Maximum Speed: 508 knots at sea level (585 mph, 941 km/h),

522 knots, 0.82 Mach No. at 10,000 feet

Range: 500 nm;

Endurance: 1 hour - with no drop tanks; (typical flight time 50 minutes)

4. The Highs and Lows of Pilot Training

Just prior to my eighteenth birthday in September 1949, I was summoned to Sheffield in Yorkshire for a medical examination prior to being drafted into the Army for 2 years of National Service. On September the 15th I received my medical certificate saying I was "Grade 1". That sounded pretty good, but at the same time I was told that I had failed the medical with "flat feet" and ordered to join the navy or the air force. I chose the air force and arriving at RAF Padgate in Lancashire, I was soon being ordered around vociferously by lance-corporals, corporals and sergeants. I expected that I would spend my two years in the air force doing something fairly dreary but hopefully useful, like being trained as a motor mechanic.

However, after marching up and down the parade ground for a few days, I accidentally heard a rumour that a small number of National Service people were being trained as pilots. So I asked the lance-corporal in charge of our hut about it. I had never been interested in aeroplanes, but it sure sounded more interesting than anything else I would be called on to do during my National Service. However the lance-corporal had never heard about it, so he referred me to the sergeant, who referred me to the Adjutant, who referred me to the Commanding Officer of the Station, who did indeed know of the scheme. So he arranged for me to attend the next round of Aptitude Tests in London the following week, and I emerged as one of 16 from a hundred applicants chosen for pilot training.

Summary of Pilot Training in the RAF 1949 - 1951

1. The total training period prior to joining a fighter or bomber squadron was 2 years. In my case it was my whole National Service period from October 1949 to September 1951.

2. The first 5 months was in "Ground School" which consisted of basic service training, including parade drills, shoe shining and belt buckle shining, plus lectures on the theory of flying such as aeronautics, meteorology and navigation. For this period I was at RAF Wittering. Then my first 200 hours flying training was at RAF Cottesmore.

3. Basic Flying Training was 100 hours, while average dual instruction before going solo was 10 to 12 hours. A first solo consisted of takeoff, climbing to 1500 to 2000 feet, going around and landing, taking straight off again, then repeating four or five times. This was followed by learning the aircraft's capabilities such as stalling and spinning characteristics, including how to recover from these; navigational exercises, and forced landing exercises simulating engine failure. This was in the Percival Prentice for our course, whilst throughout the flying training we were also given classes and exercises intended to develop us as "officers".

The Percival Prentice side by side training aircraft

4. Advanced Flying Training was 100 hours of similar exercises to the above but on an aircraft with greater power and livelier handling characteristics - the North American Harvard for us.

North American Harvard advanced trainer
with tandem seating, pupil in front seat

5. After gaining one's wings and becoming officers it took about 30 flying hours to convert to the aircraft one was most likely to end up on in a squadron. In my case this was the Gloster Meteor 4 twin engine jet fighter. It was of course a big change from piston engine to jet. As well as the increased power and speed, one of the other important characteristics of the jets at that time was the extremely slow response to throttle change, making formation flying, for example, quite challenging. For me this took place at RAF Driffield in East Yorkshire.

6. The final period of instruction at the end of the 2 years was 30 hours of "Operational Conversion", which involved not a change in aircraft, but learning the rudiments of using

one's aircraft as a weapon, and the teamwork required to work with other aircraft in a squadron. This was at RAF Stradishall, again on Meteor 4s.

So I started my flying training at Cottesmore in 1950 on the lumbering but very safe Percival Prentice with its side by side seating. The kind of initial exercises that were carried out included: use of the control column – moving it backwards raises the elevator on the tailplane and the aircraft climbs (assuming there is sufficient power set to do so); moving the control column forwards causes the plane to dive. Moving the control column to the left moves the left aileron up, increasing the drag on that wing and dropping it so that the aircraft turns left; flying "straight and level" – that is getting used to the "feel" of the control column required just to maintain a given constant speed and altitude; climbing and descending – mainly learning the effect of the throttle (power) on the rates of climb and descent, and learning the limits of the aircraft; turning while maintaining a constant altitude - the increased drag of a wing when the control column is moved sideways to initiate a turn also causes the plane to lose height, so to maintain altitude increased throttle and/or pulling back on the control column is also required.

The coordination of different actions required in a simple turn like this can remain a challenge to many pilots for some time.

Other exercises included stalling – fairly early on in one's flying training it is necessary to know and experience the limitations of the particular aircraft, especially the minimum speed that will keep it in the air (the "stalling speed"), and then to have demonstrated – at a safe altitude – what happens when the aircraft does stall, and how to recover. In theory the recovery process is simple – increase speed by moving the stick forward and increase the power. Of course the plane loses height in this procedure, so it's best not to stall near the ground. Takeoff and landing practice and "circuits" – after a mere 5 or 6 hours of flying with an instructor, it is customary to fly round and round the airport doing nothing but taking off, climbing to 1500 or 2000 feet, turning back into the circuit, landing, then without stopping going round again.

Then of course there are many other procedures and check lists to observe before and during any flight, including: checking the weather, informing the control tower of one's flight plan, start up, taxiing and pre-take off check lists, take off itself, navigation from A to B, how to position oneself in the airport circuit and prepare the aircraft for the final approach, and finally the landing and taxying to the parking position. As already indicated, while it is desirable to land as slowly as possible to minimize the landing run, there must always be a safety margin between the approach speed and the stalling speed.

First Solo – sometimes one's first solo occurs while carrying out circuits as above, when the instructor unexpectedly stops the plane on the runway after a landing, jumps out and shouts "Right, you do it on your own now!" I achieved my first solo in a modest 12 hours of flying, and 6 months later, after just 100 flying hours, we all thought we knew everything there was to know about flying, as we graduated to the Advanced Course on the much livelier North American Harvard with its tandem seating.

The Harvard did not have pressurisation, nor did we have oxygen masks, so the typical maximum altitude used for exercises was 10,000 feet. But when I heard another trainee had flown the Harvard up to 18,000 feet, I accepted the challenge to try and beat this. So at the next opportunity – when officially carrying out solo aerobatics – I climbed to 20,000 feet, the last 5,000 feet being at the laborious limit of the aircraft's capability. By this time I was suffering from anoxia (lack of oxygen) and not thinking straight. As I had already used up nearly all my scheduled time in the air I decided blurrily to get down as quickly as possible by stalling the aircraft and putting it in a spin. In this situation the aircraft falls like a heavy leaf, so very quickly I was down to 10,000 feet. I was still not thinking entirely rationally when I had another idea - to put to the test a rumour that the Harvard would recover from a spin on its own if you just took your hands off the controls. (Normally one needs to push the control column forward to increase speed, and then correct the spin by levelling the wings.) Anyway I tried sitting back and waiting to see what happened, and thankfully the Harvard righted itself. After landing I was able to gloat to my colleagues about my altitude record, hoping that the instructors did not hear about it.

I had a closer call from losing my place in the course (one way or another), after achieving what I claimed to be a low altitude record. On a solo low level exercise where one flies around the countryside at low level using particular navigation skills (theoretically not below 50 feet – or was it 200 feet?) I got carried away with the excitement again, and decided to fly as low as possible through the many fields I was traversing. Coming to the boundary of one field, I saw a gap through the trees and decided to go through this without climbing over the trees. Unfortunately power lines and telephone lines emerged too late on the other side of the trees, and I went straight through them - apparently with no ill effects. Arriving back at base, I taxied to where the ground crew were waiting for me to jump out but leave the engine running, for the next pilot to take over. However the ground crew signalled for me to cut the engine, but stay in the cockpit. I saw some of the ground crew rush off and then return with mops and rags and buckets of water and start scrubbing the wings. I saw then that they were cleaning off blood and sheep's wool from the wings. Another group of ground staff were crowding round the front of the aircraft and I saw them rushing off with a handful of short lengths of telephone wire that apparently had got stuck in the oil cooler under the engine cowling. Thus the ground crew were able to save me from having to explain to my instructor these dire consequences of my very low flying. However I did still end up getting a reprimand for the gouges in the propeller blades caused by the telephone wires, necessitating a new propeller.

Graduation as pilots with "Wings", 42 Pilots Course,
RAF Cottesmore, 1951

We celebrated our graduation from No. 7 Flying School after 12 months at Cottesmore on Wednesday, April the 11th, 1951. I believe one reason I was not thrown off the course for "average pilot skills" was my sporting involvement during this period. The services regard such achievements quite highly, so I think it helped that I represented the RAF Station in badminton, basketball, cricket, cross country running and tennis.

At the end of this course with 200 hours experience, including flying on instruments only, we emerged as Officers and Pilots with "Wings". Then we were dispatched for Jet Conversion.

5. How to Become a Jet Pilot

203 Advanced Flying School, RAF Driffield and Carnaby, Yorkshire

As the runway at RAF Driffield in Yorkshire was not long enough for the Meteor, all our flying was carried out at the nearby airfield of Carnaby. I will never forget my initial reaction of surprise at the dilapidated look of the single seater F4s lined up at Carnaby - most of them seemed to have half the rivets in their wings popped or missing. Our enthusiasm was further slightly dampened during our technical ground training when we learnt of some of the aircraft's eccentricities such as stability problems of significant longitudinal shift of centre of gravity caused by use of ammunition and/or fuel. Also we learnt that in those days of unsophisticated fuel control the reaction to throttle movements was not only very slow, requiring great anticipation by the pilot, but opening or closing the throttle too quickly would actually put out the engines completely - which I was to experience first-hand very soon!

In addition we were not exactly encouraged by the stories told us by the student pilots who were already part way through their course about the many accidents that occurred with Meteors, including 3 student pilots killed just a week previously when the instructor leading a formation at low level pulled up too suddenly so that the other aircraft in the

32

formation continued straight into the cliffs at Scarborough. It should be realised that during our training, and even when fully qualified pilots on squadrons, we were told almost nothing officially about accidents that were occurring all around us in the RAF, so it was quite an eye-opener when I read the statistics revealed in J. J. Halley's book.

Pilots converting to Meteors 4s at 203 Advanced Flying School, RAF Carnaby, Yorkshire, 1951

Mid-way through the 2 month conversion course at Driffield, I was at 30,000 feet in a "battle formation" of widely spaced Meteor 4's with an instructor leading three students. We were heading roughly south towards Hull along the coast about 50 kilometers from Carnaby. Obviously because I was not concentrating sufficiently (probably admiring the view), I dropped a long way behind the others.

I accelerated carefully to catch up. Suddenly I was catching up too fast, so to avoid whizzing past the instructor I slammed both throttles shut. That was a mistake. Certainly I avoided embarrassing myself in full view of the instructor, but now I was quickly slipping behind the formation again, so up went the throttles again. However this time there was no response from the engines, because I had extinguished both of them.

I radioed the instructor to let him know I was no longer part of his formation, and that I was turning back towards Carnaby. I was now a glider pilot with no gliding experience; well, not from 30,000 feet. During our training with instructors on the Prentice and Harvard, it was standard practice for the instructor to pull the throttles back at maybe 3000 feet altitude over the Lincolnshire countryside and shout to the pupil, "You have lost your engines – find a field to land in!" However my present situation in the meteor was different in a number of ways from the piston engine training experience - such as the altitude, the distance from base, the much greater rate of descent of the plane as a glider, and of course no instructor to start up the engines again when things got out of hand. This made me extremely nervous. But I wasn't panicking (yet) because theoretically I should be able to relight the engines, albeit not till I reached a much lower altitude.

I explained the situation to the Control Tower at Carnaby airfield and settled down to a speed of around 170 knots, at which speed the rate of descent was about 2,500 feet per minute. The next thing I had to work out was whether I would make it back to the airfield (if the engines did not relight), or whether I should be looking out for a suitable field in which to make a belly landing, or indeed whether I might be forced to bale out - a frightening thought! I knew that the Derwent engines were not likely to be restarted above 15,000 feet, so I had a wait of 6 anxious minutes gliding from 30,000 feet down to 15,000 feet. But at least during this time I was able to establish that I had covered more than half the distance back to base, so at least it looked promising that I could reach the airfield at Carnaby.

As I passed through 15,000 feet I carried out the relighting procedure on the port engine: check engine windmilling speed at about 1500 rpm, throttle one third open, LP fuel cock on, HP fuel cock off, press and hold the relight button; after 5 seconds open the HP cock while still holding down the relight button. The engine was now supposed to relight and the rpm increase so that the relight button could be released and the throttle closed fully until the engine settled down at normal idling rpm and temperature, then normal throttle position could be resumed. Unfortunately the engine did not relight.

I followed the same procedure on the starboard engine with the same result, that is, no result. So I informed the Control Tower and asked for step by step instructions for relighting an engine in case with my limited experience I had forgotten something. I followed these instructions, (which I think were the same as I had already tried), but again the engines would not start.

By now I was getting close to the airfield at about 10,000 feet, still descending rapidly of course, sweating profusely, and with legs like jelly. I agreed with the Control Tower not to try again to relight the engines, but to concentrate on getting down in one piece on the Carnaby runway. I asked for any advice they might have as to how I should try to position myself for the landing. Normally you are at a downwind position parallel to the runway at 1500 feet for a standard landing procedure – when you have engines to control your descent. In this case, to allow for my rapid descent, I was told to get to the downwind position at 5,000 feet, where I should put my wheels down - hoping there was enough hydraulic pressure for that operation - then continue to carry out a normal 180 degree turn to land.

I turned out towards the coast to lose height before turning back, and after further moments of panic when I thought I had gone too far out to sea before turning, I did in fact get back downwind at the recommended altitude. However I could see that at my present rate of descent (without wheels down), I would barely make it to the runway. In other words I would certainly not make it if I added the considerable drag of wheels down. So I continued gliding down and turning much sooner than normal until I was lined up with the runway. Then at the last moment, I selected undercarriage and flaps down, and touched down perfectly on the runway, everything in one piece, and rolling quietly to a stop just off the runway.

Of course I wasn't congratulated by my superiors for my brilliant airmanship instead I was reprimanded (again), this time for not being able to relight the engines - and of course for putting the engines out in the first place. As it turned out, I was told afterwards by the technicians that at least one of the engines' relighting circuits was faulty.

The next episode describes another incident not entirely of my own doing, which again nearly ended my career in the Air Force.

6. How to Become a Fighter Pilot

226 Operational Conversion Unit, RAF Stradishall, Suffolk

An Operational Conversion Unit (OCU) prepares pilots for operational missions of a specific aircraft type, in particular how best to exploit the performance of the aircraft as a weapon of war. Just before my 20th birthday I was with a new course of pilots at Stradishall OCU waiting for the Wing Commander to enter the room with some encouraging words of welcome. As he arrived he glared at everyone and blurted out to the whole gathering, "Get your bloody hair cut!" I don't remember what else he said.

Nearing the end of the two month course, I was being given a final check of my flying capability in the two seater Meteor 7, with an instructor in the back seat, and myself in the front seat. Everything went fine up to the point when we arrived back in the circuit at Stradishall, when the instructor suddenly cut the port engine and exclaimed, "Carry out a single engine landing!" I did not have time to work out whether he had really cut the engine (by turning off the HP fuel cock) or whether he had just pulled back the port throttle to an idle condition, because I was fully occupied just keeping the aircraft straight with right rudder, and remembering the procedure for a single engine approach and landing. In fact the downwind checks and aircraft speeds of

150 knots downwind and 130 knots final approach were hardly changed from normal, apart from needing an engine speed of at least 13,000 rpm compared to 8,000 rpm for a normal approach. However it was more critical than normal not to let the speed get too low because of the difficulty of recovering on one engine, and not to put the flaps fully down until the last moment before landing, because of the increased force needed on the rudder to counteract the asymmetric thrust as the aircraft speed reduced and the drag increased.

I was more or less comfortably settled on the final approach at 140 knots and was just about to select full flap (I can't remember now whether I actually completed this action) when the next instruction came from the back seat, "OVERSHOOT!" In other words I was to imagine that for some reason we were not able to land, and I was to climb away on one engine to make another circuit and landing. As it happened, I had carried out this very exercise myself several times in the single seater Meteor 4 both at Carnaby and at Stradishall, so I expected no problems.

No such luck this time. I opened the starboard throttle fully, attempted to hold altitude, and made to raise the undercarriage and flaps while waiting for the speed to increase to 180 knots and start a climb away. But to my dismay I found that on this aircraft even with maximum force I could not reach the full rudder position that I knew would be necessary to counter the massive asymmetric thrust. As the Meteor 7 started to roll to the left the next instruction came from the back seat, "I HAVE CONTROL!"

Soon after landing I was instructed to be in the Wing Commander's office at 3pm sharp. I knew what for - it definitely wasn't to be told to get a haircut.

I entered the Wing Commander's office with some trepidation, the feeling worsening as I saw the flight commander, and my recent instructor, both there with serious expressions. After some forgettable preliminaries the Wing Commander said, "We have decided that you have not made the grade in this operational unit and you will be taken off the course and your Pilot's Wings revoked."

I was dumbfounded. And after I recovered from the initial shock I blurted out, "I am dumbfounded."

I said "Why should I be taken off the course?" knowing full well why. I stuttered that the reason I had difficulties controlling the Meteor 7 in the extremes of single engine flight was my short legs. After a few moments of blank faces, I explained that the rudders on the Meteor 7 were further away from the pilot's seat than the rudders on the Meteor 4, and that I had no problems on the single seater, which was after all the operational aircraft I was to be using. And of course, now that I realised I had this problem on the Meteor 7, I could always put some sort of cushion behind me to be able to reach full rudder.

Then I played my trump card (a fairly low one that could easily have been over-trumped). I stated that surely it would be a gross mistake to preclude me from the course after such enormous effort and expense the British Government had spent on my training. And to stop me at the final hurdle, after nearly 2 years of being a reasonable if not brilliant pilot, just did not make sense.

And so I argued with the three officers for an hour or more until finally the Wing Commander very reluctantly agreed that I would not be precluded and I would be able to graduate as a fully qualified fighter pilot.

7. Life on a Fighter Squadron

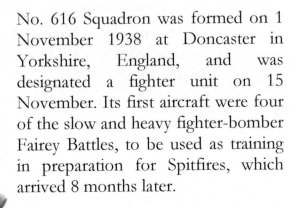

No. 616 Squadron was formed on 1 November 1938 at Doncaster in Yorkshire, England, and was designated a fighter unit on 15 November. Its first aircraft were four of the slow and heavy fighter-bomber Fairey Battles, to be used as training in preparation for Spitfires, which arrived 8 months later.

During the first part of the Battle of Britain in 1940, 616 Squadron moved to the south of England and operated over Dunkirk during the evacuation, later flying sweeps over the rest of occupied France. In July 1942 the squadron was equipped with high altitude Spitfires.

On the 12th of July 1944, 616 Squadron became the first and only allied unit to be equipped with jet aircraft during the war, and on the 27th of July the squadron flew the first operational sortie by a Meteor when it attacked Flying Bombs (V1's) launched against southern England. In February 1945 a detachment was sent to Belgium, and at the beginning of April the whole squadron moved to the Netherlands, beginning ground attack missions on 16 April. The war ended a few weeks later, and the squadron was disbanded on 29 August 1945.

On 10 May 1946 the squadron was reformed, and began to recruit personnel for an Auxiliary Air Force night fighter unit on 5 June, back at RAF Finningley. In October 1946 it received de Havilland Mosquito trainers, but it was January 1948 before the first operational aircraft arrived. It was redesignated a "Home Defence" day fighter unit in 1948, and began to acquire Meteors in January 1949, flying these until disbanded on 10 March 1957.

In September 1951, I was excited and proud to be able to join the elite 616 Squadron, which was happily based at Finningley near my home town of Doncaster, Yorkshire. I was one of the first national service pilots to join a fighter squadron, and I was certainly the first to join 616, and was the youngest amongst a select group of experienced World War II pilots.

At the time I believe that the Royal Air Force Fighter command consisted of 20 full time regular squadrons (who could be assigned duty anywhere in the world), and 20 part time auxiliary squadrons - RAuxAF - who were primarily assigned to home defence. A pilot of an auxiliary squadron was committed to attend every Thursday evening (generally for solo night flying exercises), together with a full week-end attendance, primarily for squadron operational exercises, often involving other squadrons and air forces. In addition, the whole squadron would spend 2 weeks each year carrying out exercises at an overseas base, such as Germany, Gibraltar and Malta.

This part time regime meant that during my 3 years with 616 squadron, I was also able to attend Leeds University, and get a degree in Mechanical Engineering.

Pilots of 616 South Yorkshire Squadron,
Royal Auxiliary Air Force, 1952

At the end of November after just 2 months with the squadron, I decided to miss flying for 3 weeks while I concentrated on studying for my first serious University examinations. After the examinations, I turned up at Finningley in the week before Christmas, looking forward to getting back to serious flying. But with the operational program that week already under way, I was given the honour of transporting our Flight Commander to West Raynham in Norfolk, where he was to spend the week end partying with old friends.

As he climbed into the back of one of our Meteor 7s with his weekend bag on his knees, I climbed into the front seat as pilot, and we set off. As we crossed over The Wash with Kings Lynn coming up on the right it was such good visibility that I could make out the location of the airfield about 40 miles ahead. I called the control tower asking for a direct approach to the runway in use, which was 025 degrees. A "direct approach" is one where a beeline for the final approach path is made, dispensing with the downwind and crosswind legs of the formal circuit. Gradually descending from our cruising altitude and reducing airspeed, I reached an ideal point on the long approach path at 190 knots with a quarter flap selected and 10,000 engine rpm.

Final checks for landing were carried out – airbrakes in, undercarriage down at 170 knots, fuel contents checked (enough for overshoot if required – 50 gallons), 8,500 engine rpm, flaps half, three green lights showing that all three wheels were down and locked, brake pressure OK, speed reducing to 130 knots – O No! Somehow the speed had dropped below 130, and I was descending too fast. In the short time that I had not been flying I had forgotten the intense concentration that is required every second of an approach and landing. There was a yell from the rear cockpit, but no shout of "I have control!", the usual response from a back-seat instructor, because the Flight Commander had his weekend bag on his knees precluding him from such an activity.

Because we were still doing 115 knots and the actual stalling speed was about 90 knots I thought I had a good chance of retrieving the situation and immediately opened up the throttles to maximum power. However once the speed gets down below 130 knots on the Meteor it is quite difficult to recover speed without losing height; so my corrective action turned out to be too late, and we sloshed down into a ploughed field, about 750 yards short of the beginning of the airfield. I closed the throttles and held my breath (I don't think I shut my eyes).

The only positive aspect of this disaster, (apart from the fact that we were both not yet dead), was that I was perfectly aligned with the runway, so following a bumpy ride through ploughed fields and fences, and clipping a concrete radar emplacement just short of the airfield, we finally arrived, travelling down the centerline of the runway just as though it had been a quite normal landing. It was all silent in the back seat as I continued to taxi to the parking spot, and pulled in at the place indicated by the ground staff. I kept the engines running with the intention of taking off straight away once my passenger had got out, so as I saw he was on the ground with his bag, I waved farewell to him and opened the throttles to start to move away to prepare for a take off back to Finningley. That was when the panic on the ground started.

Several ground crew ran in front of me waving their arms like mad, insisting I stop and cut the engines. I pulled up, stopped the engines, and got out of the aircraft - and surveyed the damage. Most of the underside skin of the Meteor 7 fuselage and wings was missing, (and I thought of the Wing Commander at 226 OCU Stradishall who had obviously been right after all when he said I shouldn't be flying).

As I was wearing only underwear beneath my flying suit, I was confined to quarters in the Officer's Mess while the partying got under way that evening. But someone took pity on me. They found me a uniform that nearly fitted, and I was off down to the drinking, dancing and cigar smoking. The dancing turned out to be quite enjoyable for me, in spite of the shame and embarrassment I should have felt. This was because the uniform I was given had three stripes on it, so it wasn't long before the ladies were queuing up to dance with the very young looking Wing Commander.

Again, when the statistics were finally published in J. J. Halley book in 1999, I found myself to be in good, no, bad company with 200 other Meteor pilots between 1945 and 1957 who also wrote off a Meteor during the approach and landing phase for one reason or another, including 60 of these accidents being caused by undershooting the runway, in a similar way to my episode, (with 17 of these occurring when practising flying on one engine).

In fact the Gloster Meteor did seem to be more than usually susceptible to accidents, for example, during my first full year with 616 Squadron (1952), the RAF and RAuxAF lost 3

Meteors written off every week, and a Meteor pilot was killed every 4 days.

In the next chapter I will state some of the characteristics of the Meteor 8 which may have contributed to some of the many accidents with this aircraft. Following that, I will describe some more of my own experiences relating to these characteristics.

Ground crew of 616 Squadron preparing a Meteor with ventral and wing tanks for the long flight home from Ta Qali, Malta

8. Gloster Meteor Characteristics

1. On takeoff you had to take care not to get the nose wheel too high while still on the ground because it was easy to hit the tail on the runway.

2. Like any aircraft, a stall could initiate a spin, but in a Meteor a spin could sometimes be prefaced by rolling upside down, making recovery quite tricky, especially as both hands were often required to overcome the heavy forces.

3. The Meteor 8 had rocket-powered ejector seats, but the Meteor 7 did not, so the not so straightforward instructions for abandoning the 2 seater read: "Jettison the hood; dive over the inboard edge of the wing; do not drop out from an inverted aircraft. If the aircraft is spinning, dive out on the side away from the axis of spin. After the hood has been jettisoned, the remaining hood strut forms a considerable obstruction on the right side of the front cockpit, so the front pilot should leave by the port side if possible".

4. Severe buffeting could be felt at high Mach Numbers – different on different aircraft. It was said that the buffeting and various control problems would get worse with the age of the aircraft as its smooth painted surface deteriorated.

5. If the speed or altitude was allowed to get too low on approach to landing, a surprising amount of power was required to recover and get back on the ideal glide path. This was especially so on one engine when a large amount of rudder was also needed, (everything becoming even more exaggerated on an overshoot).

6. It was essential to maintain correct trim on the elevator at high speeds, to obviate the possibility of sudden excessive elevator forces. Similarly, during a high speed run at lower altitudes, it was important not to have the elevator trim set in too high a position, because this would add to the forces caused by a sudden pull-up, creating possible structural damage.

7. The rudder trimmer was awkward to operate.

8. A positive point was that the Meteor had a high rate of climb for its time, getting to 30,000 feet in under 6 minutes from sea level. With air brakes out and the throttle closed, a high rate of descent of over 15,000 feet per minute was also possible.

9. On the Meteor 7 with no pressurisation, misting of the windscreen could occur at the lower altitudes of a high speed descent.

10. The single hydraulic pump on the Meteor was driven by the starboard engine. If this failed, the windmilling engine

may or may not provide enough power to lower flaps and undercarriage, but would certainly not give enough power to raise them again. However there was an emergency hand pump.

11. Sustained inverted flight was safe for only 15 seconds, due to the possibility of fuel and oil starvation.

12. Flying on one engine at low speeds was not straightforward - for example the overshoot procedure for abandoning a landing was different according to which engine was being used:
    flying on the starboard engine only, "raise flaps and undercarriage, and increase speed to 180 knots before climbing away (at 180 knots)":
    flying on the port engine: "raise flaps but leave the undercarriage down, increase speed to 165 knots before climbing away initially at 165 knots".

13. The throttle needed to be opened and closed very smoothly to avoid an engine flame out, (with a somewhat improved fuel control in the very latest versions).

14. At high altitudes the high pressure fuel cock could freeze in the open position, (usually freeing itself with reduction in altitude).

15. There could be an indication of oil pressure failure at high altitude, which would generally prove to be false on descent to a lower altitude.

16. The maximum allowed landing weight was close to the condition with full fuselage fuel tanks, so that if fuel was in the ventral tank, or in wing tanks, this had to be used up, or the tanks jettisoned, before landing.

17. Aerobatic and similar manoeuvres were not permitted with fuel in the ventral tank.

18. When carrying wing tanks, sustained high rates of descent were not advised, because of the possibility of tank collapse due to the lag of pressure equalization in the tanks.

19. Action to relieve jamming of undercarriage lever: "Throttle back starboard engine and reduce speed. Select flaps and/or dive brakes in and out, until hydraulic system is exhausted. If this doesn't work, close down the starboard engine completely, and operate dive brakes again".

20. After selecting wheels down, the starboard undercarriage came down first. If the port undercarriage was slow coming down, the undercarriage locking mechanism could operate prematurely, locking one wheel down and one wheel up. Action: "Operate the undercarriage emergency lock over-ride lever, so you can select undercarriage up, then down again".

21. As mentioned, the "stretched fuselage" of the Meteor 8 and the Meteor T7 contained an extra fuel tank of 95 gallons in front of the main tank, feeding by gravity into both compartments of the main tank. The main fuel tank of 325 gallons, in the fuselage behind the cockpit, was divided into two equal compartments, front and rear, the two compartments being connected by a balance cock, which was normally closed, but could be manually opened by the pilot. The port engine was fed from the front compartment of the main tank, and the starboard engine from the rear compartment, this arrangement causing some peculiar fuel management problems, especially when fuel levels were low. For example in a steep climb, the sloping fuel level in the front compartment could drop below the fuel feed point, starving the port engine, while in a steep descent, the starboard engine could die from lack of fuel.

22. If flying on one engine, the situation was more complicated. For example, <u>in level flight</u>: using the starboard engine only - open the balance cock. Using the port engine only - open the balance cock above 250 knots, close it below 250 knots. <u>In a climb</u>: using the starboard engine - balance cock open; using the port engine only - close the balance cock. <u>In a descent</u>: the opposite to the climb requirements.

23. At full power on just one engine, the fuel flow was greater than the flow from one compartment to the other through the open balance cock.

24. If there was fuel in the ventral tank, it was advisable to make frequent use of it because of the propensity for its inward vent valve freezing, especially following the use of the wing tanks at high altitude.

25. Finally, two characteristics which were never officially acknowledged - at least the information was never passed down to the pilots. It was rumoured that if you selected wheels down with the dive breaks still out, some unpredictable instability and partial lack of control could result.

It seems that this lack of stability could have been caused by a spiralling airflow around the aircraft being initiated by the wheels coming down one at a time, the starboard wheel first. This would normally correct itself when the port leg came down, but could be exacerbated, and even made impossible to correct if the dive brakes were out when the undercarriage was selected down. The aircraft could then become unstable in a variety of ways.

For example when this happened to me, the aircraft would no longer turn left, so (after lots of trying various manoeuvres), my only recourse was to keep carrying out right hand turns to land. This is discussed further in the next chapter.

26. In a high speed dive, control loads became extremely heavy, so that much higher forces than expected were required for recovery. Unfortunately this was not

officially acknowledged for many years, so there continued to be many fatalities - officially labelled *"unexplained dive into the ground"* or similar, (the unofficial jargon calling this a "phantom dive"). You will have read in the opening chapter of this book my personal experience of this type of event.

9. More Near Death Experiences

Dozing off on a long flight

Everyone in an Auxiliary Squadron looked forward to the time of the year when 2 weeks was spent on operational flying exercises overseas. While with 616 Squadron I enjoyed times in Celle, near Hanover in Germany (right next to the East German border), at Gibraltar (right next to Spain), and in Malta. Not the least of the excitement were the long range flights from our UK base to the destinations, involving careful planning and navigation for such short range aircraft. On one such exercise to Gibraltar, we had to land at Marseille for refuelling. On the second leg, the effects of the long lunch, and especially the French wine, caused me to doze off at 30,000 feet. Luckily I woke up before reaching the waters of the Mediterranean after losing only a few thousand feet, and was able to regain my position in the loose formation without the leader noticing (I think). On a sadder note, while at Gibraltar that year we lost one of our newer pilots who inexplicably dived into the sea from a high altitude.

Running out of Fuel

The Meteor was capable of carrying extra fuel tanks, one under the fuselage (the ventral tank) and two wing tanks. The wing tanks held 100 imperial gallons each but were normally only used for special long distance occasions because they diminished the performance significantly. The ventral tank, holding 175 imperial gallons (800 litres), was used more often, but it did pose the threat of almost certain fire in a belly landing, and aerobatic manoeuvres were precluded until it was empty. Both ventral tanks and wing tanks could be jettisoned if necessary, for operational or emergency reasons.

We would normally fly without any extra tanks, and then the endurance of the Meteor was just one hour on the 330 imperial gallons in the main fuselage tank (1500 litres). Civil airliners carry enough fuel to fly to an alternative airfield many miles away should there be problems with the original destination. In the Meteor the programmed flight time was typically 50 minutes, so if we missed our first landing due to the weather or just bad flying, there was only just enough fuel to allow one more attempt to land. This is perhaps one reason why there were over 50 Meteors written off, and at least 10 deaths, due to "Running out of fuel".

Because of the requirement for fighter aircraft to be always flown to their limits of speed, range and endurance, there were many times when the refuellers would tell the pilot afterwards that the fuel tanks had been virtually empty on landing. I ran out of fuel once, when the engines stopped on the runway, just after landing.

Collisions

Everyone can imagine the thrill and appreciate the skill

required for close formation flying, especially formation aerobatics, which only the very best pilots can carry out. People marvel at how close the aircraft seem, and wonder if they are close as they look. In fact they are. Typically the spacing is just a few metres, and total concentration is required to keep in position in even just straight and level flying. It is perhaps surprising that there are not more accidents during these exercises. There were of course a few collisions while formation flying, (and more than once I was amazed I did not crash into an adjacent aircraft), but there were probably more collisions during practice combat exercises, such as dog fights.

The thrill of piloting a fighter was the continual flying at the limits of the aircraft's capabilities of speed, engine power, manoeuvrability, fuel constraints and weather situations. So every flight where there was some element of operational reality, there were inevitably risks. I always enjoyed such exercises where our squadron was pitted against other squadrons. Our gun sights were fitted with 16mm movie cameras, so that when we pressed the firing button our attacks were recorded on film. These movies were assessed afterwards, and we were given marks for possible kills. One such exercise nearly killed me, and possibly a few others.

Typically we may have been lounging at the bar in the Mess, when without warning the order to "Scramble!" would be given over the Tannoy loud speakers. We would rush to our lockers, grab our helmets with oxygen mask and microphone and other equipment, tear out onto the tarmac shouting to the ground crew to connect up the ground batteries, (the engines could be started on the internal batteries only if they were fully charged). We would leap into the cockpit, sitting on our parachutes with straps dangling. Without carrying out any pre-start checks, the starboard engine starter button was held for 5 seconds and HP fuel cock turned half on, followed immediately with the port engine starter button and HP cock. When reasonably sure that both engines were started the external batteries were shooed away and chocks away signalled. The HP cocks were then used almost as throttles, as they were fully opened and we taxied at speed to the end of the runway.

With safety harness and parachute straps still dangling we would take off in semi-formation, (dangerous enough!), and if not already with the correct flight of two or four or more, we would join up as quickly as possible after takeoff. We would then be given instructions from the control tower such as, "Intercept bandits approaching Sheffield at 25,000 feet". And then we might remember to do up our safety harness and parachute straps.

On one particular exercise, our enemy was a flight of B29 bombers of the United States Air Force that were at 25,000 feet. When our radar controllers reckoned the time was right, we were scrambled, and our flight of four Meteor 8s climbed in the direction given to us by fighter control radar. As we reached 28,000 feet we spotted the amazing so-called box formation of 24 Flying Fortresses below us. The B29s relatively close formation created the equivalent of the

English infantry square, so that every angle of attack from marauding fighters was covered by their many gun stations.

We turned and dived to attack. The only possibility I could see was to concentrate on one of the B29s on the outer edge of one of the boxes. I did have experience of simulated dog fights with other fighters of similar speed and manoeuvrability to the Meteor, but I was caught off guard by the slow speed of the Fortresses. I found I had totally misjudged my attack, and was closing at such a rate that I had to spend the next few seconds weaving and dodging between the B29 formations just trying to avoid a collision, never managing once to get even one shot in. I never did hear what the B29 pilots thought of our blundered attack.

Air Shows

It is well known that some of the riskiest exercises that any pilot can take are at an air show, or practising for an air show, where the capabilities of pilots and aircraft are demonstrated (shown off) to the public. The problems are that unusual manoeuvres are often carried out that are not within the normal experience of the pilots. But even more critical is the requirement for these to be carried out where the public can see them, at low level, where there is little chance to recover should something go wrong – which it often does.

While with 616 Squadron I was involved in a simulated ground attack on a grass airfield near Doncaster in

Yorkshire, where an airshow was being held. I was piloting one of several Meteors diving steeply one after the other over the airfield (simulating dropping bombs), when I hit the turbulence (slipstream) of the Meteor in front of me, at about 500 feet. My plane was immediately tossed around almost out of control, but I did manage to regain control just before I hit the ground. It must have looked quite spectacular to the crowd.

An even more spectacular episode occurred three years later during one of the annual airshows at Bristol, when I was with 501 RAuxAF Squadron at RAF Filton. A colleague of mine and I decided we would demonstrate the speed range of the Meteor to the crowd at the Filton airfield. He was to fly at maximum speed (over 500 mph) just to one side of the runway at 50 feet altitude, while I was to fly in the opposite direction, also at 50 feet on the other side of the same runway as slowly as possible (about 150 mph), so that we would just miss each other over the crowd. Of course this required some planning and practice beforehand, but we thought that we had it about right by the time of the show day.

When it was our turn to demonstrate, we both took off and positioned ourselves ready for the run in. Throughout my slow speed run with gear and flaps down, I was hoping my colleague was going to miss flying straight into me, thus creating a typical airshow accident. Even if we did not collide I thought he had chosen the more spectacular routine, and was sure he would get the plaudits of the crowd as he climbed rapidly away after his high speed run.

Just after passing each other perfectly over the crowd, I slammed open the throttles to climb away, selecting gear and flaps up at the same time, and although I was momentarily concerned (scared) when the engines did not respond for a few seconds, I was eventually able to increase speed and altitude and climb away safely.

On getting out of the cockpit after landing, I was surprised to be greeted by an enthusiastic crowd telling me what a wonderful show I had put on. It turned out that when I slammed open the throttles right over the crowd, the engines fuel system had barely coped, causing great sheets of flame to spurt from the engine as it faltered and nearly flamed out, so all the attention was on my slow moving aircraft, rather than the usual focus on my high speed colleague.

Aircraft Characteristics

The dangerous locking up of the controls of the Meteor at high speed, and how it apparently caused the deaths of many pilots, has already been described. It has also been mentioned that the Gloster Meteor suffered from stability problems.

It was on one of my last flights in a Meteor while with 501 Squadron at Filton in Bristol, that I experienced one of these peculiarities for myself. In those days we had no idea of the problems the Meteor had in its development, and we only ever heard rumours about the many accidents, so if anything unusual occurred our superiors always suggested that it was the pilot's fault.

Returning from an exercise at high altitude in a Meteor 8, I descended rapidly at 350 knots with dive brakes out, dropping from 20,000 feet to 2,000 feet in just over a minute, quickly slowing to 200 knots and levelling out over the Bristol Aircraft Company works, heading west at 1500 feet in the ideal downwind point to the right of the east-west runway. I put the flaps to one quarter and set 10,500 rpm on the engines. As the speed slowed to 175 knots I lowered the undercarriage. ("Downwind" means flying parallel to the runway preparatory to making a 180 degree turn to line up for the final approach and landing.) As the runway passed out of sight behind my left wing, I reduced the throttle to give 8,500 rpm, and moved the control column gently to the left to start turning left and descending on the cross wind leg, prior to the final approach.

But the Meteor 8 just skidded, and kept flying straight ahead. In fact as I pushed the control column more to the left the aircraft swung to the right. After a few seconds of trying to turn left, I gave up and called the control tower to indicate the difficulty I was having, and said I would fly around and try again. I could sense the disbelief in the controller's voice when I told him "I cannot turn left". So I had to get permission from the control tower to carry out a circle to the right over Bristol city because it was the only way I could go, to reposition downwind again. When exactly the same thing happened on my next circuit, I said to the control tower that I was going to climb to 5,000 feet to carry out some experiments.

I tried every possible configuration of dive brakes, flaps and undercarriage at different speeds, but to no avail – I still could not get the Meteor 8 to turn left. The next suggestion was to drop the ventral fuel tank which was attached to the under belly of this aircraft. So I flew over the middle of the Bristol Channel as the safest place to jettison the tank. Unfortunately that made no difference either. As I was fast running out of fuel, I called the Filton control tower, and told them I would attempt a landing by carrying out a right hand circuit, rather than the usual left hand circuit. Apart from the fact that every action I took had to be carried out by always turning right, I did land safely, and reported my interesting experiences to the Squadron Commander.

Of course I was not believed, or at least I was told it was unbelievable, and that I must have had too much to drink the night before.

Naturally I was disappointed that I did not get a proper chance to discuss seriously the reasons for this behaviour of the Meteor 8, especially because of my many years of experience flying the Meteor, as well as my experience as a Senior Flight Test Engineer with Bristol Aero Engines, flying in the English Electric Canberra and Avro Vulcan bombers, programming and analyzing test flights, both for them, and several European fighter aircraft as well.

10. A Page of Statistics

The following statistics are from the book by Mr. James J. Halley M.B.E. "Broken Wings" published by Air Britain (Historians) Limited 1999, soon after Air Ministry archived statistics from the Cold War period were released.

SOME OF THE CAUSES OF ACCIDENTS TO THE GLOSTER METEOR 1945-1957 IN FIGHTER COMMAND (Royal Air Force and Royal Auxiliary Air Force)

1. <u>Unexplained Dive into the Ground</u>: 80 write-offs, 80 deaths

2. <u>Collisions</u>: 80 write-offs, 50 deaths

3. <u>Single-engine Practice</u>: 38 write-offs including 12 Meteor 7s with both pilots killed, 33 deaths

4. <u>Bale Outs</u>: 100 write-offs (100 bale out attempts), 30 deaths

5. <u>Approach and Landing</u>: 200 write-offs including 60 undershoots and 25 wheel collapses, 12 deaths

6. <u>Running out of Fuel</u>: 56 write-offs, 11 deaths

<u>Total 1945-1957</u>: nearly 800 write-offs and 400 deaths

There were 329 Meteor pilots killed during the time I was flying Meteors, the worst year being 1952 (my first full year with 616 Squadron), when on average a Meteor pilot was killed every 4 days.

APPENDIX 1

Extracts from Pilot's Notes for Meteor 8 – 1955

2nd Edition

A.P. 2210 H & J.—P.N.

PILOT'S NOTES

FOR

METEOR 8 & 9

PREPARED BY DIRECTION OF THE MINISTER OF SUPPLY

J. R. C. Helmore

PROMULGATED BY ORDER OF THE AIR COUNCIL

J. H. Barnes

PILOT'S EXTERNAL CHECK LIST

Start at the port side of the nose and work clockwise around the aircraft.

Item	Check
Cockpit hood (port side)	Condition Absence of cracks Security
External hood clutch release	In locked position
Ground/Flight switch	FLIGHT
Fuel low pressure warning lights	On
Ventral and wing drop tanks fuel transfer lights	On
Nose wheel mechanical indicator	Protruding
Nose wheel	Extension of oleo. Security of mudguard. Tyre for cuts and creep. Valve free. Condition of doors and fairings.
Cockpit hood (starboard side)	Condition Absence of cracks Security
Starboard centre section	Condition of leading edge
Starboard nacelle	All cowlings secure
Starboard undercarriage	Condition of doors. Brake lead secure. Tyre for cuts and creep. Valve free. Pump and ignition isolating switches on
Starboard mainplane	Condition of leading edge Security of drop tank (if fitted)
Starboard navigation light	Condition
Starboard aileron	External control lock removed Condition and movement of aileron and balance tab

Item	Check
Starboard mainplane	Condition of upper and lower surfaces
	Condition of flap and air brakes
	Picketing ring removed
Underside of fuselage	Security of panels. Condition of glass over identity lights
Starboard side of fuselage	Condition
External aerials	Secure
Fin	Condition
Starboard tailplane	Condition
Starboard elevator	External control lock removed
	Condition
Rudder	External control lock removed
	Condition
Tail light	Condition
Port elevator	External control lock removed
	Condition
Port tailplane	Condition
Emergency skid	Condition
Port side of fuselage	Condition
	Picketing ring removed
Port mainplane	Condition of upper and lower surfaces
	Condition of flap and air brakes
	Condition of landing lamp
	Picketing ring removed
Port aileron	External control lock removed
	Condition and movement of aileron and balance tab
Port navigation light	Condition
Pressure head	Cover removed
Port mainplane	Condition of leading edge
	Security of drop tank (if fitted)

Item	Check
Port nacelle	All cowlings secure
Port undercarriage	Condition of doors
	Brake lead secure
	Tyre for cuts and creep. Valve free. Pump and ignition isolating switches on
Port centre section	Condition of leading edge
Ventral drop tank	Secure

PART II

HANDLING

43. **Cockpit checks**

Ejection seat safety pin	Removed and stowed
Dinghy pack lanyard	Clipped to life-saving waistcoat
Parachute straps	Clipped on
Harness straps	Clipped on
Oxygen	Pipe attached to mask
Emergency oxygen	Pipe attached to point on mask pipe

Start at left-hand side of cockpit and work round to right.

Oxygen selector (if fitted)	Correctly set
No. 1 engine L.P. cock	On
No. 1 engine H.P. cock	Off
Fuel balance cock	Off
Internal hood clutch release	Up (engaged)
Pneumatic pressure gauge	Total supply and delivery to each wheel brake
Undercarriage emergency override	Down
Rudder and elevator trim controls	Full and correct movement
V.H.F. channel selectors	Off
Air brake lever	In
Cockpit pressurising lever	COLD
Battery isolating switch	On
L.P. pump switches	Off
Landing lamp switch	Off

Flap lever	Exhaust accumulator then return to neutral
Undercarriage selector lever	Down
Wing tanks and bomb jettison lever	Forward
Ventral tank jettison lever	In
Undercarriage indicator	Green lights on Check bulb changeover
Undercarriage warning light	Out
Fuel gauges	Note readings
Hood jettison handle	In
Oxygen regulator	Contents and delivery
Emergency oxygen control	Plunger in
Undercarriage emergency air control	Plunger in
Switches on panel	Off (or as required)
No. 2 engine L.P. cock	On
No. 2 engine H.P. cock	Off
Crowbar	In position
Hydraulic handpump	Pump flaps up and down
Harness release	Check operation
Windscreen de-icer hand pump	Operate and retract plunger

46. **Starting the engines**

(i) Either engine may be started first.

(ii) Have a ground starter battery plugged in and the Ground/Flight switch set to GROUND. It is important that the ground starter battery is fully charged and switched on the whole time during the starting sequence, as the engine needs assistance from the starter motor to accelerate up to idling r.p.m.

(iii) Press the appropriate starter pushbutton and release it after two seconds.

(iv) When the undercarriage lights dim or after a maximum period of five seconds, move the H.P. cock to the half open position. When r.p.m. increase, the cock should be moved slowly to the fully open position. The engine should accelerate to idling speed with the throttle closed. The jet-pipe temperature may momentarily exceed the idling limit but it should settle down to not more than 500°C. The throttle must not be opened before idling r.p.m. is attained.

(v) If the H.P. cock is moved too quickly from the half to the fully open position, resonance and overheating may occur. If excessive jet pipe temperatures and resonance persist, close the H.P. cock to stop the engine. Sufficient time must elapse in order to drain off excess fuel before restarting is attempted.

(vi) Repeat the procedure for the other engine and allow both engines to accelerate to idling r.p.m. Before removing the ground starter battery the Ground/Flight switch must be set to FLIGHT.

(vii) In the event of an engine failing to light up proceed as follows:—

(a) Turn off the H.P. cock.

(b) Have the appropriate ignition and priming pump isolating switches set off.

(c) Ensure that the impeller has stopped turning; wait until the fuel has stopped draining from the nacelle and then dry out the engine by carrying out the starting cycle with the H.P. cock in the off position.

(d) When the impeller has again stopped turning, have the ground crew remove any surplus fuel from the jet pipe.

(e) Have the ignition and priming pump isolating switches set on.

(f) Start the engine as in sub-paras. (iii) to (v) above.

(viii) Simultaneous starting of both engines is not permissible, but when for operational purposes it is necessary to start the engines with minimum delay, the starter pushbutton of the second engine may be pressed not less than five seconds after the starter pushbutton for the first engine has been released. The starting sequence then becomes:—

(a) No. 2 engine starter button—press and release.

(b) When the undercarriage lights dim or five seconds after releasing No. 2 starter button turn No. 2 engine H.P. cock half on.

(c) No. 1 engine starter button—press and release.

(d) When the undercarriage lights dim or five seconds after pressing No. 1 engine starter button turn No. 1 engine H.P. cock half on.

(e) Ease both H.P. cocks to the fully on position.

(ix) If during starting of No. 2 engine a severe hammering is encountered, it is due to air in the hydraulic system, and should disappear when one of the hydraulic services is operated.

47. **Checks after starting**

Engine idling speed	3,300 to 3,700 r.p.m.
Oil pressure	5 lb./sq. in. idling minimum
Jet pipe temperature	500°C. idling maximum
Engine fire warning lights	Out

48. Checks before taxying

Start at right-hand side of cockpit and work round to left.

Hood	Close
Windscreen demister booster switch	On
Mark 4F compass master switch	On
Pressure head heater switch	On
Warning horn master switch	On
Oxygen	On and reaching mask
Flight instruments	Check and set
Flaps	Operate and check with indicator
Air brakes	Operate and check visually
V.H.F.	Select set and channel
Cockpit pressurising control	PRESS
Pneumatic pressure gauge	Check 450 lb./sq. in. total supply, or sufficient and increasing. (Check brakes as soon as possible after taxying)

49. Taxying

(i) Initial response to the throttles is slow, and the aircraft is not easy to turn without assistance from the brakes.

(ii) When taxying, fuel consumption is high, being about one gallon per minute, at idling r.p.m., for each engine.

FINAL CHECKS FOR TAKE-OFF

TRIM   ... ELEVATOR : $1/2$ DIV.
                             NOSE DOWN
            RUDDER : NEUTRAL

AIR BRAKES ... IN

FUEL   ... CONTENTS
            H.P. COCKS ON
            L.P. COCKS ON
            L.P. PUMPS ON
            BALANCE COCK CLOSED

FLAPS   ... UP OR $1/3$ DOWN

INSTRUMENTS... CHECK AND SET

OXYGEN   ... ON AND REACHING
                             MASK

HOOD   ... CLOSED
            TOGGLES IN LINE

HARNESS   ... TIGHT AND LOCKED

51. **Take-off**

NOTE.—(a) When conditions make the use of the shortest possible take-off run essential, the brakes should be applied when the aircraft is aligned on the runway and the throttles opened gradually to take-off r.p.m. The brakes should then be released. If the brakes will not hold at 12,000 r.p.m. they should be regarded as unserviceable.

(b) If it is necessary to check any of the engine instruments, this should be done against brakes prior to take-off.

(i) Open the throttles smoothly to take-off r.p.m.

(ii) The aircraft accelerates rapidly but there is no tendency to swing. The rudder becomes effective at about 60 knots.

(iii) The nosewheel can be eased off the ground at approximately 90 knots and the aircraft flown off at 110-120 knots, with one-third flap, or 115-125 knots with flaps up, depending on load.

(iv) At maximum weight, with ventral and wing drop tanks fitted, one-third flap should always be used to reduce the unstick speed. The nose can be raised at 110 knots and the aircraft flown off at about 130 knots.

(v) Brake the wheels momentarily before raising the undercarriage and, to avoid risk of damage, the undercarriage should be locked up before the speed reaches 175 knots.

(vi) The flap lever should be returned to NEUTRAL when the flaps are up.

(vii) The safety speed is 150 knots (155 knots on aircraft with large intakes), but should an engine cut immediately after take-off, the aircraft may be controlled at lower speeds, provided that prompt corrective action is taken.

NOTE.— Should the cockpit pressurising control lever be set to PRESS prior to take-off, kerosene fumes may occasionally be blown into the cockpit. These should clear soon after becoming airborne.

52. **Climbing**

(i) *Operational climb*

Commence the climb using 14,550 r.p.m. A governor on the engine-driven fuel pump restricts the r.p.m. to 14,550 for take-off, but, with the throttle fully opened, r.p.m. may increase progressively to 14,700 with increase in altitude. However, a close watch should be kept on the jet pipe temperatures which must not be allowed to exceed 680°C. (700°C. above 20,000 feet). If surging, recognised by a muffled detonation from an engine, is experienced, the throttle should be closed slightly until the surging ceases. The following indicated climbing speeds are recommended:—

Sea Level	...	...	...	300 knots
10,000 feet	...	.....	...	280 knots
20,000 feet	...	...	...	260 knots
30,000 feet	...	...	...	235 knots
35,000 feet	...	...	...	220 knots
40,000 feet	...	...	...	200 knots

(ii) *Normal climb*

If maximum rate of climb is not essential, the climb should be made at 14,100 r.p.m. maintaining the same speeds as above.

(iii) Outside air temperature affects the climb performance considerably. Under standard conditions, and without drop tanks fitted, using full power, a climb to 40,000 feet can be made in approximately 12 minutes. This is reduced to 11 to 11½ minutes when the large type intake is fitted.

(iv) If the cockpit has not already been pressurized the warning horn should sound at about 9,000 feet. The control lever should then be set to PRESS and this should silence the horn. If after this the horn sounds at any time, it indicates that the cockpit differential pressure is low, and the cockpit altimeter should be checked by comparison with the main altimeter. (See table of relative readings in paragraph 26 (ii)).

PART II—HANDLING

53. General flying

(i) *Controls*

    (a) *Elevators.* The elevators are effective throughout the speed range. The elevator trimming control is positive and very effective and the aircraft is easy to trim under most conditions of flight. At high altitude with the aircraft at the aft C.G. (i.e. without ammunition) the elevator stick forces are light, but there is no tendency for the aircraft to tighten in turns.

    (b) *Ailerons.* The ailerons, if fitted with geared tabs only, will become heavy to operate at high I.A.S. On aircraft fitted with spring tabs, the ailerons are more effective at high I.A.S., but become less effective at low I.A.S.

    (c) *Rudder.* The rudder forces are light at low speeds but moderately heavy at high speeds.

    (d) *Air brakes.* The air brakes open fully at any speed. At high speeds they are very effective, and the deceleration will cause the pilot to be thrown forward, if the harness straps are not tightly adjusted.

(ii) *Changes of trim*

Increase in power causes a slight nose-up change of trim, and increase in speed an appreciable nose-up change of trim. Because of the latter, it is advisable to trim into a dive to avoid the risk of excessive "g" on pulling out. Operation of the flaps, undercarriage, or air brakes cause little change of trim.

(iii) *Snaking*

Snaking may occur, particularly between 200-250 knots with low power, air brakes out.

(iv) *Engine controls*

There is little or no risk of flame extinction at altitude, provided that the throttles are moved smoothly and not too rapidly. The throttles may be fully closed at any height, and idling r.p.m. are normally between 5,000 and 7,000 at 200 knots.

54. **Flying at reduced airspeed**

Reduce speed to 150 knots and lower one-third flap.

55. **Flying with hood open**

The aircraft can be flown with the hood open at speeds below 260 knots without discomfort. No attempt should be made to close the hood in flight, as there is a risk that this may damage the seal.

56. **Flying in conditions of severe turbulence.**

(i) The recommended speed for flying in conditions of severe turbulence is 215 to 225 knots up to the height at which this speed corresponds to a speed of 0.5 M, i.e., up to about 20,000 feet; but any speed between 195 knots and 450 knots may be used if operationally necessary.

(ii) At higher altitudes the aim should be to fly at a speed of 0.5 M provided the I.A.S. does not fall below 195 knots.

(iii) At very high altitudes a speed of 195 knots should be maintained, any small risk due to compressibility effects at speeds above 0.5 M being accepted.

57. **Cockpit pressurisation**

The minimum engine r.p.m. to maintain cockpit pressure above 40,000 feet is approximately 11,000 on either or both engines. Throttling back above 40,000 feet should therefore be carried out with care. Should the cockpit pressure warning horn sound, engine r.p.m. should be increased.

61. Stalling

(i) The approximate stalling speeds, power off, are:—

	Undercarriage and flaps up knots	Undercarriage and flaps down knots
At maximum landing weight (14,700 lb.)	100	90
Full internal fuel and ammunition	105	95
Full internal fuel, full ventral tank, and ammunition ...	110	100
Full internal fuel, full ventral and wing drop tanks, and ammunition	120	110

(ii) Stall warning is given by gentle buffeting, which starts 10 to 15 knots above the stall, becoming more marked as the stalling speed is approached.

(iii) The stall is not well defined. As the control column is moved back and speed decreased, the buffeting becomes more pronounced, until, with the stick fully back, it is severe. There may be some pitching, particularly with the flaps and undercarriage down, and also some lateral rocking. Recovery is straightforward.

(iv) With the air brakes open the buffeting will be more severe but the stalling speeds are only two or three knots higher.

(v) When sufficient "g" is applied, warning of the approach of a stall is given by buffeting, and continued rearward movement of the control column will cause the buffeting to become more severe until at the stall the nose of the aircraft drops. There is no marked tendency for either wing to drop. Recovery is straightforward.

62. High speed flying

(i) The high mach number characteristics vary between individual aircraft. Generally speaking the behaviour at high mach numbers becomes worse with age, and with deterioration of the external finish. Mach meter instrument errors may be considerable as the aircraft reaches its critical mach number.

(ii) The characteristics stated below are typical of an aircraft in good condition.

(iii) On most aircraft there is little or no compressibility effect up to a mach number of about 0.79. After this, a strong nose-up change of trim may develop quickly. This is more pronounced at altitudes below about 25,000 feet. Around this height snaking may be experienced.

(iv) On aircraft which have only geared aileron tabs, aileron buffet may commence at 0.8 M; between 0.8 M and 0.82 M aileron snatching occurs with a tendency for either wing to drop. At this stage the ailerons are heavy and only moderately effective. Rudder helps to a limited degree to hold up a wing.

(v) When both spring tabs and geared tabs are fitted, lateral control may be maintained up to about 0.83 M, at high altitudes only, thereafter either wing may drop. At high mach numbers these ailerons are slightly less heavy than the geared tab type.

(vi) Application of small amounts of "g" induce the compressibility characteristics at mach numbers below those stated above.

(vii) *With wing drop tanks.* When wing drop tanks are carried aileron buffeting and wing dropping may occur at about 0.72 M, particularly if "g" is applied.

(viii) *Use of the elevator at high mach numbers.* It is recommended that elevator forces should not be trimmed out at speeds above 0.8 M. At heights below about 25,000 feet this may involve using full nose-down trim. If, after trim has been applied, the speed is reduced, even to 0.79 M the aircraft will become very nose-heavy as the effects of compressibility diminish. The aircraft must, therefore, be retrimmed. Nose heaviness occurs rather quickly if speed is reduced quickly, e.g., when air brakes are used.

(ix) It is recommended that pilots investigate the high mach number effects of an aircraft progressively, until they are aware of its characteristics.

PART II—HANDLING

63. Aerobatics and spinning

(i) The following minimum speeds are recommended:—

Roll	250 knots
Loop	350 knots
Roll off top	350 knots
Climbing roll	400 knots

(ii) In manoeuvres in the looping plane, height gained or lost may be considerable. An ample margin should therefore be allowed.

(iii) *Spinning*

Practice spinning is permitted only with the clean aircraft, or with the ventral tank fitted but empty. The spin should not be entered below 25,000 feet, and recovery action must be taken before the end of the second turn. Entry may be either from a straight stall, or from a turn. Air brakes have little effect on the spin, but, if used, should be left in the out position until recovery is complete.

The aircraft will normally enter the spin by first rolling onto its back, and then dropping its nose. Behaviour in the spin varies widely between aircraft, and between spins on the same aircraft. A "rough ride" must be expected: pitching, changes in rate of rotation, flick rolling, and snatching of the stick from side to side, are all characteristics which can occur to varying degree in various spins. Except in isolated cases, however, the stick will snatch over to the inside of the spin.

Normal recovery action is effective, but should not be taken while the aircraft is inverted at the beginning of the spin. Prior to recovery, speeding up of rotation, and steepening of attitude may be experienced, especially in spins entered from a turn. Heavy control forces must be expected; a two-handed force will normally be required to centralise the stick. Care must be exercised to prevent a spin in the opposite direction after rotation has ceased.

NOTE.— The negative "g" traps in the main tank ensure a supply of fuel sufficient for about 15 seconds inverted flight; this must not be exceeded owing to the possibility of oil starvation. If a ventral drop tank is fitted aerobatics must not be carried out unless it is empty. If wing drop tanks are fitted, aerobatics, are prohibited.

FINAL CHECKS FOR LANDING

FUEL   ... CONTENTS
                      BALANCE COCK CLOSED

AIR BRAKES ... IN

BRAKES   ... CHECK PRESSURES
                      OFF

UNDER-
  CARRIAGE ... DOWN AND LOCKED
                      THREE GREEN LIGHTS

FLAPS   ... $1/3$ DOWN
                      FULLY DOWN ON
                          FINAL APPROACH

HARNESS   ... TIGHT AND LOCKED

65. Approach and landing

The turn on to the final approach should be made at approximately 140 knots, and the airfield boundary crossed at the following speeds:—

Condition	*Speed*
With less than 100 gallons	105 knots
*Maximum landing weight 14,700 lb. ...	110 knots

*With ammunition, drop tanks empty, and approximately 280 gallons remaining.

Without ammunition, drop tanks empty, and approximately 340 gallons remaining.

The initial approach should be made 15 knots above these figures. No increase in speed is necessary when landing with an empty ventral tank, but the above speeds should be increased by 5 knots when landing with empty wing drop tanks.

66. Instrument approach

The following speeds together with the appropriate flap and approximate power settings are recommended for use during instrument approaches with the undercarriage lowered:—

	R.P.M.	Flaps	Airspeed
Pattern	11,500	One-third	150 knots
Final	11,500	Two-thirds	125 knots
Glide Path	10,000	Two-thirds	120 knots

67. Going round again

(i) The power required and the fuel used will depend on when the decision to go round again is taken. If the decision is made on the approach at about 300 ft. the use of 12-13,000 r.p.m. will give satisfactory acceleration and control. Going round again under these conditions requires a total of approximately 15 gallons of fuel. Going round again after touchdown is straightforward using full power initially. In this case a total of 30 gallons of fuel should be allowed to complete the circuit and landing.

(ii) In all cases:—

(a) Open the throttle smoothly to give the required r.p.m.

(b) Raise the undercarriage and flaps fully.

(c) After reaching 150 knots, commence climbing.

68. Braking

After touchdown, when the nosewheel is on the ground, gentle continuous braking pressure may be applied. The pressure may be increased as the aircraft ground speed decreases.

69. Checks after landing

Pneumatic pressure	Sufficient for taxying
Flaps	Up
Pressure head heater switch	Off
Cockpit pressurising lever	In COLD
Windscreen de-mister booster switch	Off

70. Stopping the engines

On reaching dispersal, stop the engines by turning off the H.P. cocks. Then, after the impellers have stopped, switch off the low pressure pumps.

71. Checks after stopping the engines

Electrical services	All off
Battery isolating switch	Off
Chocks	In position
Brakes	Off
Ejection seat safety strap	Insert through blind handle and secure with safety pin.

LIMITATIONS

73. Flying limitations

(i) (a) The aircraft is designed for the duties of a single seat fighter; intentional spinning up to two turns is permitted when the aircraft is clean, or when the ventral tank is fitted, provided that it is empty. Aerobatics are prohibited when carrying wing drop tanks, full or empty, or when carrying a ventral drop tank unless it is empty. The carriage of R.P. is permitted but until further trials are completed the carriage of bombs is prohibited.

(b) During high speed runs at sea level, if the aircraft is out of trim (nose up) and a heavy pull force is applied to the control column, excessive "G" may easily be induced in the subsequent climb—resulting in structural damage. The elevator stick force must be trimmed out up to the maximum speed attained in the run, and pull forces applied with care.

(c) For similar reasons as outlined in (ii) above, a speed of 400 knots must not be exceeded during ground attack manoeuvres. An angle of dive of 45° must also not be exceeded.

(d) Unless Mod. 1610 is incorporated, a rate of descent of 5,000 feet min. should not be exceeded when empty wing drop tanks are carried, as there is a risk of collapse due to an insufficiently rapid equalisation of the pressure difference. A tank collapse does not affect the trim.

EMERGENCY CONTROLS AND EQUIPMENT

74. Undercarriage, flaps, and air brakes emergency operation

(i) Any of the above may be operated by the handpump, after the desired selection. Little resistance is felt when the handpump is used, until the selected service is fully extended.

(ii) The emergency air system for lowering the undercarriage is operated by pulling the T-handle (56) on the cockpit starboard wall. The undercarriage will then lower irrespective of the position of the selector lever. It is recommended that this system be used for the undercarriage, any accumulator pressure being retained for lowering the flaps.

(iii) If the undercarriage selector lever jams, it may be due to hydraulic back pressure sticking the rotary valve. Relief is provided by exhausting the hydraulic system. The starboard engine should be throttled back, speed reduced, and the air brakes or flaps operated until the selector lever is free.

(iv) If, after selecting DOWN, the port undercarriage is slow to lower, the ground-lock may come into action on the compressed oleo-leg, and the selector lever will be locked down with the port leg locked up. It will be necessary to operate the override before the lever can be freed The lever should then be selected DOWN in the usual way

PART IV—EMERGENCIES

EMERGENCY HANDLING

82. Engine failure during take-off

(i) With flaps one-third down and undercarriage down, the safety speed is 150 knots (155 knots on large intake aircraft). If, however, after an engine failure, corrective action is taken quickly and about 10° of bank towards the live engine is applied, the aircraft can be controlled at any speed above the "unstick" speed. Care must be taken not to apply excessive bank.

(ii) Raise the undercarriage and allow the speed to increase to safety speed. Commence climbing, but allow the aircraft to continue accelerating up to 200 knots, then raise the flaps at a safe height.

83. Engine failure in flight

(i) In the event of engine failure which can be attributed to a mechanical defect, immediate action should be:—

    (a) H.P. cock   ...   .   Off

    (b) L.P. cock   ...   .   Off

    (c) Low pressure pump ...   .   Off

    (d) Balance cock   ...   .   Open

(ii) In case of fire in an engine:—

Proceed as in (i) above reversing the order of (a) and (b), and reduce speed if possible before operating the engine fire-extinguisher.

(iii) Where engine failure has occurred due to flame extinction, do not turn off the L.P. cock, as this may cause damage to the fuel pump and B.P.C.

84. Restarting an engine in flight

(i) *Derwent Mk. 8*

    (a) Attempting to relight an engine at heights above 15,000 ft. is not recommended. Although a successful relight may be achieved if it is attempted immediately flame extinction occurs, it may, if unsuccessful, jeopardise the chances of a relight below 15,000 ft.

    (b) Ensure that the L.P. cock and the L.P. pump are on and that the H.P. cock is closed, then:—Set the throttle one-third open, reduce windmilling r.p.m. to 1,000-1,200 by decreasing the airspeed. Press the relighting button and after five seconds turn on the H.P. cock, keeping the button pressed. When r.p.m. reach 2,000 release the relighting button and close the throttle fully. When the engine is running satisfactorily at normal jet pipe temperature, open up to the desired r.p.m.

    (c) If an engine fails to relight, the H.P. cock must not be left on for more than 30 seconds and at least one minute should elapse between attempts to relight, to allow the engine to "dry out". The next attempt should be carried out at a lower altitude with a wider throttle opening.

    (d) If the above method fails, no attempt should be made to relight the engine using the normal starting method.

85. Single-engined landing

    (i) Maintain a speed of at least 150 knots while manoeuvring with the undercarriage and flaps up.

    (ii) A single-engined landing presents no difficulty. Lower one-third flap and the undercarriage as on a normal circuit, maintaining a speed of 140 knots until the decision to land has been made. (145 knots on large intake aircraft.) Then lower the flaps fully as required and use the approach speeds quoted in paragraph 65.

    (iii) With the wheels and one-third flap down, going round again on one engine at the speeds recommended above using full power involves no loss of height. If No. 2 engine has failed, the undercarriage and one-third flap should be left down for the circuit; in this condition the aircraft will climb away satisfactorily.

When the weather was too poor for flying
the tradition at 616 Squadron was to have a champagne party

APPENDIX 2 - ALL RECORDED ACCIDENTS
CAUSING WRITE-OFFS TO GLOSTER METEORS
IN THE ROYAL AUXILIARY AIR FORCE & ROYAL AIR FORCE
OCTOBER 1945 TO DECEMBER 1957

Statistics from "Broken Wings" by J.J.Halley

ISBN 0 81530 290 4 published by Air-Britain (Historians) Limited

No.	Date	Type	Serial No.	Unit	Place	Official Cause Bold type indicates pilot(s) killed
entries that are <u>underlined</u> indicate an apparent uncontrolled dive into the ground, often from cloud or similar. The possible cause of this kind of accident is described in Chapter 1.						
1	15.10.45	F3	EE347	1335 CU	UK	Ran out of fuel – force landed
2	20.11.45	F3	EE316	1335 CU	UK	*Missing on unauthorized night flight*
3	28.11.45	F3	EE313	1335 CU	UK	*Failed to recover from spin*
**3 write-offs and 2 deaths in 1945**						
4	02.01.46	F3	EE335	74 Sqdn	UK	*Crashed after low run and upward roll*
5	15.01.46	F3	EE390	124 Sqdn	UK	*Collided with EE392 in formation*
6	15.01.46	F3	EE392	124 Sqdn	UK	*Collided with EE390 in formation*
7	01.02.46	F3	EE448	222 Sqdn	UK	*Dived into ground during aerobatics*
8	08.03.46	F3	EE344	74 Sqdn	UK	*Hit tree during dummy attack on train*
9	23.04.46	F3	EE293	245 Sq	UK	*Stalled on single engine approach*
10	09.05.46	F3	EE518	Glosters	UK	*Broke up in high speed turn*
11	17.05.46	F3	EE363	56 Sqd	UK	Hit trees during formation take off
12	29.06.46	F3	EE311	WEE	Can.	Fuel feed failure, ditched
13	01.07.46	F3	EE295	222 Sqdn	UK	*Flew into ground in fog*
14	02.07.46	F3	EE312	A&A EE	UK	*Failed to recover from spin test*
15	18.07.46	F4	EE538	Glosters	UK	*<u>Dived into ground out of cloud</u>*
16	19.07.46	F3	EE346	74 Sqdn	UK	Engine failure, force landed in field
17	19.07.46	F3	EE444	CFE	UK	Undercarriage locked up, belly landed
18	09.08.46	F3	EE466	EFS	UK	Engine failure, force landed in field

19	23.08.46	F3	EE362	56 Sq	UK	Engine failure on approach, crashed
20	12.09.46	F3	EE301	263 Sqdn	UK	Engine fire in air, force landed
21	13.09.46	F3	EE490	CGS	UK	*Broke up during high speed slow roll*
22	10.10.46	F3	EE338	PRDU	UK	*Crashed during turn after take off*
23	24.10.46	F4	EE579	AFDS	UK	Wings wrinkled in flight
24	11.11.46	F3	EE343	263 Sqdn	N.Sea	*Missing*

21 write-offs and 13 deaths in 1946

25	17.03.47	F3	EE422	222 Sqdn	UK	*Dived into ground out of cloud*
26	25.03.47	F3	EE296	226 OCU	UK	Heavy landing, undercarriage collapsed
27	22.04.47	F4	RA394	Glosters	UK	*Crashed on attempted overshoot*
28	23.04.47	F3	EE446	CFE	Germ.	Lost both engines, belly landed
29	05.05.47	F4	EE578	CFE	UK	Fuselage broke up in flight, baled out
30	16.06.47	F3	EE411	266 Sqdn	Germ.	*Crashed during low level turn*
31	07.07.47	F4	RA418	2 FP	UK	Ran out of fuel, belly landed
32	08.07.47	F3	EE333	74 Sqdn	Germ.	Engine fire in air, belly landed
33	25.07.47	F4	EE477	EFS	UK	Elevator malfunction, skin buckled
34	05.08.47	F4	EE467	EFS	UK	Went round after undershoot, belly landed
35	14.08.47	F4	EE409	92 Sqdn	UK	Undershot on landing
36	24.09.47	F3	EE353	74 Sqdn	UK	*Crashed on single engine approach*
37	07.10.47	F4	EE457	222 Sqdn	UK	Overshot landing, caught fire
38	23.10.47	F3	EE385	56 Sqdn	Germ.	*Elevator failed, broke up at low level*
39	05.12.47	F3	EE404	263 S	UK	Engine failed on overshoot
40	18.12.47	F3	EE297	245 Sqdn	UK	Ran out of fuel, belly landed in field
41	18.12.47	F3	EE303	245 Sqdn	UK	Ran out of fuel on approach, belly landed

42	18.12.47	F3	EE364	56 Sqdn	Neth.	Ran out of fuel, belly landed in field
43	22.12.47	F3	EE450	222 Sqdn	UK	Caught fire when battery connected

19 write-offs and 5 deaths in 1947

44	15.01.48	F3	EE394	222Sq	UK	Overshot landing
45	28.01.48	F3	EE281	226 OCU	UK	Undershot landing
46	09.02.48	F3	EE245	266Sq	UK	Mechanic sucked into engine
47	12.02.48	F3	EE399	66 Sqdn	UK	Crashed while landing on one wheel
48	26.02.48	F4	EE475	266 Sqdn	UK	Heavy landing, undercarriage collapsed
49	16.03.48	F4	RA482	38 MU	UK	*Dived into ground soon after take off*
50	19.03.48	F3	EE453	92 Sqdn	Germ.	*Crashed during ground attack practice*
51	19.03.48	F4	RA488	257 Sqdn	UK	Crashed during forced landing after engine failure
52	03.04.48	F3	EE294	266 Sqdn	UK	Belly landing after engine exploded
53	29.04.48	F4	VT108	RAE	UK	Ran out of fuel on approach, crash landed
54	04.05.48	F4	VT126	245 Sqdn	UK	*Flew into ground under low cloud*
55	12.05.48	F4	EE493	EFS	UK	Stalled on approach and hit ground
56	04.06.48	F4	RA477	CFE	UK	*Dived into ground from cloud*
57	10.07.48	F4	VT143	92 Sqdn	UK	Heavy landing, undercarriage collapsed
58	27.07.48	F4	RA445	257 Sqdn	UK	Engine caught fire, damaged airframe
59	05.08.48	F4	RA447	257 Sqdn	UK	Tyre burst on take off, swung off runway
60	26.08.48	F4	RA450	222 Sqdn	UK	*Control lost in flight, dived into sea*
61	30.08.48	F4	EE568	ETPS	UK	*Unexplained dive into ground*
62	04.09.48	F4	VT144	CFE	UK	Damaged on take off (debris),

						belly landed
63	05.09.48	F4	VW787	CFE	UK	Stalled on approach, crash landed
64	14.09.48	F4	VT172	1 Sqdn	UK	Engine exploded during taxying
65	22.09.48	F4	VT136	263 Sqdn	UK	Engine caught fire just prior to take off
66	24.09.48	F4	EE461	1 Sqdn	UK	*Collided with Tiger Moth in circuit*

23 write-offs and 7 deaths in 1948

67	05.01.49	F4	VT123	245 Sqdn	UK	*Double engine failure, crashed on landing*
68	08.01.49	F4	VT269	92 Sqdn	UK	Ran out of fuel, belly landed in field
69	13.01.49	F4	VT315	66 Sqdn	UK	Collided with another F4, pilot baled out
70	17.01.49	F4	RA453	CFE	UK	Engine exploded after takeoff, belly landed
71	27.01.49	F4	VW782	CFE	UK	*Control lost after overshoot, crashed*
72	14.02.49	F4	VT193	56 Sq	UK	Ran out of fuel, pilot baled out
73	24.02.49	F4	VW789	DFLS	UK	Landed, ran off end of runway, caught fire
74	28.02.49	F4	VT140	1 Sqdn	UK	*Missing on air to sea firing practice*
75	05.03.49	F4	RA382	A&A EE	UK	*Dived into ground from high altitude*
76	07.03.49	F4	VT116	263 Sqdn	UK	Undershot single engine approach
77	13.04.49	F4	VT340	RRE	UK	Crashed
78	19.04.49	F4	RA452	FCCS	UK	Ran out of fuel, crashed on landing
79	22.04.49	F4	VT233	222 Sqdn	UK	Abandoned in spin during aerobatics
80	13.05.49	F4	VT119	263 Sqdn	UK	Heavy landing, undercarriage collapsed
81	26.06.49	F4	RA414	263 Sqdn	UK	Overshot landing, undercarriage torn off
82	28.06.49	F4	VT148	257 Sqdn	UK	Collided with VW783, pilot baled out

83	28.06.49	F4	VW783	257 Sqdn	UK	Collided with VT148, pilot baled out
84	13.07.49	F4	RA481	222 Sqdn	UK	Stalled on approach, crash landed
85	16.08.49	F3	EE357	6 MU	UK	Ailerons fitted wrongly, crash landed
86	22.08.49	F4	VT277	66 Sqdn	Norw.	Crash landed after undercarriage failure
87	30.08.49	F4	VT137	257 Sqdn	UK	Overshot landing, ended in gully
88	02.09.49	F4	VT247	222 Sqdn	UK	*Crashed during slow roll in display practice*
89	14.09.49	F4	VT221	CBE	UK	Overshot landing
90	25.09.49	F4	VT258	63 Sqdn	UK	Undershot landing, undercarriage collapsed
91	26.09.49	F4	RA455	FIDS	UK	Stalled on landing, undercarriage collapsed
92	04.10.49	F4	VT180	1 Sqdn	UK	Engines flamed out, crash landed

This is when I joined the Royal Air Force, and began ground training for Officer and Pilot at RAF Wittering, Cambridgeshire.

93	14.10.49	T7	VW434	56 Sqdn	UK	*Flew into high ground in cloud (2)*
94	15.11.49	T7	VW448	203 AFS	UK	*Flew into fog after take off, crashed*
95	21.11.49	F4	VT320	257 Sqdn	UK	*Hit tank during practice ground attack*
96	23.11.49	F4	VT124	245 Sqdn	UK	*Collided with a Proctor aircraft, crashed*
97	23.11.49	T7	VW476	226 OCU	UK	*Stalled on approach, crashed*
98	25.11.49	F4	VT238	43 Sqdn	UK	*Hit hill in bad visibility (with VT276)*
99	25.11.49	F4	VT276	43 Sqdn	UK	*Hit hill in bad visibility (with VT238)*
100	14.12.49	F4	RA451	74 Sqdn	UK	Undershot single engine landing
101	19.12.49	F4	VT257	43 Sqdn	UK	Crashed during attempted overshoot
102	21.12.49	F4	EE594	1 of	UK	Stalled on approach, crash

				AM		landed

36 write-offs and 13 deaths in 1949				

103	08.01.50	F3	EE472	616 Sqdn	UK	Both engines failed, pilot baled out
104	16.01.50	F4	VT261	92 Sqdn	UK	Hit ground during single engine overshoot
105	02.02.50	F$	VW788	203 AFS	UK	*Stalled on approach, crashed*
106	28.02.50	F4	VT217	RAF FC	UK	Undershot landing, hit hangar
107	08.03.50	F4	VT314	226 OCU	UK	Wing tank hit runway on take off
108	21.03.50	F4	RA374	226 OCU	UK	Collided with VT267, crash landed
109	21.03.50	F4	VT267	226 OCU	UK	*Collided with RA374, crashed*
110	29.03.50	F4	VW277	56 Sqdn	UK	*Crashed during formation aerobatics*
111	05.04.50	T7	VW481	CFS	UK	Hit ground during single engine approach
112	12.04.50	F4	RA372	226 OCU	UK	*Crashed following an attempted overshoot*
113	13.04.50	F4	VZ410	245Sq	UK	*Spun into ground out of cloud*
114	17.04.50	F4	VT131	66 Sqdn	UK	Stalled on landing, undercarriage collapsed
115	19.04.50	F4	VT146	1 Sqdn	UK	*Collided with another F4 during aerobatics*

On 19.04.50 I began 12 months flying training on Prentices, then Harvards, at No.7 FTS Cottesmore.

116	21.04.50	F4	VT345	504 Sqdn	UK	Undershot landing, undercarriage torn off
117	24.04.50	F4	VT185	Met. Sect.	UK	*Dived into ground during snowstorm*
118	24.04.50	F4	VW287	226 OCU	UK	*Dived out of cloud, lost wing*
119	26.04.50	T7	VW440	203 AFS	UK	*Stalled on approach, crashed*
120	28.04.50	T7	WA616	1OFU	Libya	*Disappeared from cloud (2)*
121	09.05.50	F4	VT234	CFE	UK	*Unexplained dive into ground*

						out of cloud
122	14.05.50	F4	VW267	92 Sqdn	UK	*Ran out of fuel, pilot baled out unsuccessfully*
123	16.05.50	F4	VT343	257 Sqdn	UK	Abandoned take off, undercarriage raised
124	26.05.50	F4	VT173	1 Sqdn	UK	*Engine failed during single engine approach*
125	15.06.50	F4	VW785	CGS	UK	Stalled on approach, crashed
126	29.06.50	T7	WA631	73 Sqdn	Malta	Undershot runway, crash landed
127	29.06.50	T7	WA668	CFS	UK	Broke up during aerobatics, pilot baled out
128	04.07.50	F4	VT213	63 Sqdn	UK	*Flew into ground during let down procedure*
129	06.07.50	T7	VW484	245 Sqdn	UK	*Unexplained dive into ground from cloud (2)*
130	08.07.50	F4	VW265	263 Sqdn	UK	Heavy landing, undercarriage collapsed
131	09.08.50	F4	VT216	504 Sqdn	UK	Ran out of fuel, ditched near Spurn Head
132	17.08.50	F4	RA422	203 AFS	UK	Crashed on attempted single engine overshoot
133	28.08.50	F4	VT198	63 Sqdn	UK	*Stalled on approach, crashed*
134	05.09.50	T7	WA695	2 FP	Germ.	Force landed in bad weather, hit tree
135	12.09.50	T7	VZ631	257 Sqdn	UK	Belly landed after previous heavy attempt
136	14.09.50	T7	VW431	CFE	UK	*Collided with USAF F84, crashed*
137	20.09.50	F4	RA383	203 AFS	UK	Stalled on single engine approach, crash landed
138	27.09.50	T7	WA614	203 AFS	UK	*Ran out of fuel, ditched in St. Georges Channel (2)*
139	28.09.50	F4	VW292	203 AFS	UK	*Crashed on attempted single engine overshoot*
140	14.10.50	F3	EE290	500 S	UK	*Collided in formation, crashed*
141	30.10.50	T7	WA673	CFS	UK	*Broke up in unexplained dive out of cloud (2)*
142	24.11.50	T7	WA625	203 AFS	UK	Hit slipstream on approach, crash landed

143	30.11.50	F4	EE599	205 AFS	UK	*Ran out of fuel, pilot baled out unsuccessfully*
144	07.12.50	F4	RA487	66 Sqdn	UK	Lost at night, pilot baled out
145	07.12.50	F8	VZ558	74 Sqdn	UK	*Flew into ground in circuit at night*
146	11.12.50	F4	VT170	205 AFS	UK	Ran out of fuel, belly landed in field
147	21.12.50	F4	VT342	TFU	UK	*Unexplained dive into ground*
148	28.12.50	F4	RA431	226 OCU	UK	Ran out of fuel, belly landed
46 write-offs and 20 deaths in 1950						
149	05.01.51	F8	VZ449	74 Sqdn	UK	*Crashed in sea after reporting damage*
150	06.01.51	F4	EE550	615 Sqdn	UK	*Unexplained dive into ground from 20,000 feet*
151	12.01.51	T7	VW314	226 OCU	UK	Stalled on landing, crash landed
152	12.01.51	T7	WA719	205 AFS	UK	Undershot on single engine approach
153	19.01.51	F8	VZ469	43 Sqdn	UK	*Hit sea low flying*
154	25.01.51	F4	VW255	205 AFS	UK	*Unexplained dive into ground from cloud*
155	27.01.51	F4	VW312	226 OCU	UK	Skidded on ice on landing, hit another Meteor
156	01.02.51	T7	WA603	CFE	UK	Lost hood in spin, pilots baled out
157	14.02.51	T7	VW474	203 AFS	UK	*Unexplained dive into sea (2)*
158	15.02.51	FR9	VZ585	2 Sqd	Germ.	Ran out of fuel, belly landed
159	16.02.51	F8	VZ498	245 Sqdn	UK	*Ran out of fuel, crashed*
160	23.02.51	F4	VW289	226 OCU	UK	*Dived into ground after take off*
161	27.02.51	T7	WA677	205AFS	UK	*Crashed during aerobatics (2)*
162	01.03.51	F8	WA935	1 OFU	P.Gulf	*Missing on ferry flight*
163	18.03.51	F4	VZ404	504 Sqdn	UK	*Unexplained dive into ground*

164	28.03.51	F8	VZ447	CFE	UK	Caught in slipstream, undershot landing
165	10.04.51	T7	WA708	203 AFS	UK	Pilots baled out during spin
166	12.04.51	F8	VZ518	66 Sqdn	UK	*Flew into hill in formation in cloud*
167	12.04.51	F8	WA791	66 Sqdn	UK	*Flew into hill in formation in cloud*
168	17.04.51	F4	EE592	205 AFS	UK	Accidentally landed with wheels up
169	17.04.51	F8	VZ527	66 Sqdn	UK	*Broke up during low run*
170	27.04.51	F4	VT186	226 OCU	UK	Undershot single engine landing
171	30.04.51	F4	VT102	615 Sqdn	UK	*Unexplained dive into ground*
172	01.05.51	T7	WA678	CFE	UK	*Engine failure, crashed on approach (2)*
173	01.05.51	T7	WA711	205 AFS	UK	Hit ground on single engine overshoot
174	01.05.51	T7	WF786	71 Sqdn	Germ.	Lost hood and tail, pilots baled out
175	06.05.51	F8	WE933	64 Sqdn	UK	*Unexplained dive into ground from cloud*

This is when I joined 203 Advanced Flying School, Driffield, Yorkshire, for conversion to the Meteor.

176	19.05.51	F8	WA827	245 Sqdn	UK	*Engine failed after take off, crashed*
177	28.05.51	F4	VT189	226 OCU	UK	*Hit ground during air to ground firing practice*
178	29.05.51	T7	WA604	228 OCU	UK	*Sideslipped into ground on approach (2)*
179	29.05.51	T7	WA617	208 Sqdn	Cyprus	Undershot landing
180	05.06.51	F4	VT325	226 OCU	UK	Double engine failure, belly landed on airfield
181	18.06.51	F4	VT275	600 Sqdn	UK	*Collided with VT281, baled out unsuccessfully*
182	18.06.51	F4	VT281	600Sq	UK	*Collided with VT275, crashed*
183	18.06.51	F8	WB110	41 Sq	UK	*Sank to ground after take off*

184	19.06.51	F4	VT239	205 AFS	UK	*Unexplained dive into ground*
185	19.06.51	F8	VZ509	74 Sqdn	UK	*Spun into water (Norfolk Broads)*
186	20.06.51	F8	WA877	66 Sq	UK	*Broke up in air*
187	23.06.51	T7	VW438	602 Sqdn	UK	*Ran out of fuel, hit trees on forced landing*
188	24.06.51	F8	WA771	56 Sqdn	UK	Stalled on approach, undercarriage collapsed
189	26.06.51	F8	WE955	1 Sqdn	UK	Ran out of fuel on approach, belly landed
190	27.06.51	F4	VT246	226 OCU	UK	*Hit ground during air to ground firing practice*
191	27.06.51	F8	WA953	56 Sqdn	UK	*Crashed soon after take off*
192	02.07.51	T7	WA692	4 Sqdn	Germ.	Accidentally landed with wheels up
193	03.07.51	F8	VZ569	65 Sqdn	UK	*Hit by WA985, pilot baled out unsuccessfully*
194	03.07.51	F8	WA985	65 Sqdn	UK	Hit VZ569, pilot baled out
195	07.07.51	F4	EE584	504 Sqdn	UK	*Engine failed on approach, crashed*
196	10.07.51	F4	VZ418	205 AFS	UK	*Unexplained dive into ground*
197	10.07.51	F8	WE924	66 Sqdn	UK	Landed with one wheel up
198	22.07.51	F4	VT121	611 Sqdn	UK	*Unexplained dive into ground from cloud*
199	09.08.51	FR9	WB114	2 Sqdn	Germ.	Lost control in cloud, pilot baled out
200	19.08.51	T7	WF790	41 Sqdn	UK	*Dived into ground during aerobatics (2)*
201	23.08.51	F8	WA843	92 Sqdn	UK	*Lost tail during unexplained dive*
202	26.08.51	T7	WA687	614Sq	UK	Overshot landing, raised wheels
203	30.08.51	F4	VZ414	226 OCU	UK	Undercarriage collapsed on landing

This is when I joined 226 Operational Conversion Unit, Stradishall, for Fighter training on the Meteor.

| 204 | 06.09.51 | F4 | VT188 | 610 | UK | Undershot runway wiping off |

				Sqdn		undercarriage
205	10.09.51	F8	VZ510	263 Sqdn	UK	*Broke up in air (1 + 3 on ground)*
206	13.09.51	F4	VT244	203 AFS	UK	Undershot approach
207	15.09.51	F8	WB106	63 Sqdn	UK	Hit by WE869, pilot baled out
208	15.09.51	F8	WE869	63 Sqdn	UK	*Hit WB106, pilot baled out unsuccessfully*
209	17.09.51	FR9	VZ581	208 Sqdn	Cyprus	*Dived into ground after ground attack run*
210	17.09.51	T7	WF842	612 S	UK	*Unexplained dive into ground (2)*
211	25.09.51	F4	VT324	205 AFS	UK	*Unexplained dive into ground from cloud*

This is when I joined 616 Squadron, Finningley, Yorkshire on Meteor 8's. Up to now there had been 211 Meteors lost by accident, including 115 deaths of which 31 were possible "unexplained dives into the ground".

212	02.10.51	T7	WF860	71 Sqdn	Belg	Lost, crash landed
213	05.10.51	F4	VT307	203 AFS	UK	*Flew into cliffs in formation (Scarborough)*
214	05.10.51	F4	VW301	203 AFS	UK	*Flew into cliffs in formation (Scarborough)*
215	05.10.51	F8	WA774	222 S	UK	Overshot landing, hit shed
216	07.10.51	F8	WA867	222 Sqdn	UK	Failed to become airborne on take off, crashed
217	10.10.51	F4	RA416	226 OCU	UK	Hit slipstream on landing, wheels collapsed
218	10.10.51	F8	WA787	263 Sqdn	UK	*Unexplained dive into ground after take off*
219	24.10.51	FR9	VZ589	208 Sqdn	Egypt	Undershot landing, undercarriage wiped off
220	25.10.51	F4	VT278	226 OCU	UK	*Engines failed, pilot baled out unsuccessfully*
221	01.11.51	F8	VZ497	56 Sqdn	UK	*Hit by WA940 after landing, caught fire*
222	01.11.51	F8	WA940	63 Sqdn	UK	*Hit VZ497 after landing, caught fire*
223	05.11.51	T7	VZ642	CFS	UK	Hit wires and trees on approach

						to land
224	08.11.51	F8	WE950	56 Sqdn	UK	Both engines lost, belly landed in field
225	17.11.51	T7	WF876	85 Sq	UK	*Engine cut on approach, crashed*
226	20.11.51	F4	VT114	205 AFS	UK	Both engines lost on approach, belly landed
227	20.11.51	T7	WA720	205 AFS	UK	Lost control during aerobatics, both pilots baled out
228	24.11.51	F4	VW297	205 AFS	UK	*Hit Officers' Mess after roller landing*
229	30.11.51	T7	WF767	203 AFS	UK	*Dived into ground after night take off (2)*
230	04.12.51	FR9	VZ587	2 Sqdn	Germ	*Crashed into wood while low flying*
231	04.12.51	T7	WF777	202 AFS	UK	Engine cut on roller landing, belly landed
232	07.12.51	F4	VT339	226 OCU	UK	*Broke up while low flying*
233	20.12.51	F4	RA426	203 AFS	UK	Collided with VW304, pilot baled out
234	20.12.51	F4	VW304	203 AFS	UK	*Collided with RA426, crash landed*
235	20.12.51	F4	VT280	203 AFS	UK	Stalled on single engine landing, crash landed
236	21.12.51	T7	WA716	202 AFS	UK	Ran out of fuel, belly landed in field
237	22.12.51	T7	WG936	141 Sqdn	UK	*Crashed on overshoot with one engine (2)*

89 write-offs and 59 deaths in 1951

238	02.01.52	F8	WE896	1 OFU	Burma	Overshot runway on delivery flight
239	04.01.52	F3	EE332	206AFS	UK	*Broke up in high speed run*
240	07.01.52	F8	VZ453	92 Sqdn	UK	Collided with WA759, overshot belly landing
241	07.01.52	F8	WA759	92 Sqdn	UK	*Collided with VZ453, crashed*
242	07.01.52	NF 11	WD653	264 Sqdn	UK	Ran out of fuel at night, pilot baled out
243	10.01.52	F8	WE854	19 Sqdn	UK	*Hit slipstream during landing, killed man on ground*

244	20.01.52	F8	WE864	19 Sqdn	UK	Collided with WE 868, pilot baled out
245	20.01.52	F8	WE868	19 Sqdn	UK	*Collided with WE864, pilot baled out unsuccessfully*
246	21.01.52	FR9	VZ591	208 Sqdn	Egypt	*Hit slipstream landing, wheels collapsed*
247	21.01.52	T7	WG975	205 AFS	UK	*Stalled and crashed on approach*
248	12.02.52	F8	WA882	222 Sqdn	UK	*Flew into snow covered hill while low flying*
249	18.02.52	F8	WA996	64 Sq	UK	Lost tyre on take off, belly landed
250	18.02.52	F8	WE860	64 Sqdn	UK	Airfield closed by bad weather, pilot baled out
251	21.02.52	T7	WH232	20 MU	UK	*Hit ground on single engine approach*
252	24.02.52	T7	WA726	500 Sqdn	UK	*Stalled in circuit, crashed*
253	24.02.52	T7	WG948	614 Sqdn	UK	Caught fire when starter trolley detached
254	26.02.52	T7	WF831	207AFS	UK	Undershot single engine landing, hit train
255	29.02.52	F8	WE937	64 Sqdn	UK	*Unexplained dive into ground from cloud*
256	29.02.52	F8	WH342	66 Sqdn	UK	*Collided with another F8 in formation, lost tail*
257	04.03.52	F4	VT326	203 ANS	UK	*Flew into ground while low flying*
258	04.03.52	F8	WE888	56 Sqdn	UK	*Canopy failed during aerobatics, crashed*
259	14.03.52	F4	VT283	203 AFS	UK	*Hit trees on approach, crash landed*
260	19.03.52	T7	WF589	87 Sqdn	Germ.	Undershot during single engine landing
261	20.03.52	T7	VW437	229 OCU	UK	Running out of fuel, belly landed, caught fire
262	26.03.52	F4	VT129	203 AFS	UK	Undershot landing
263	27.03.52	F4	VT199	215 AFS	UK	Undershot landing
264	28.03.52	T7	VZ632	205 AFS	UK	Lost power after overshoot, belly landed

265	01.04.52	F4	VZ411	226 OCU	UK	*Control lost in cloud, crashed*
266	02.04.52	T7	VW455	203 AFS	UK	Ailerons jammed, pilots baled out
267	10.04.52	T7	WA636	IAM	UK	Lost canopy, stalled on approach, caught fire
268	12.04.52	F8	WF700	41 Sqdn	UK	Engine caught fire, pilot baled out
269	16.04.52	T7	WG986	205 AFS	UK	*Stalled on single engine approach, crashed (2)*
270	17.04.52	T7	WF878	205 AFS	UK	Skidded landing, undercarriage collapsed
271	24.04.52	F4	VW269	203 AFS	UK	*Control lost in cloud, dived into sea*
272	24.04.52	T7	WA665	205 AFS	UK	*Broke up soon after take off (2)*
273	24.04.52	NF 11	WD712	29 Sq	Germ	Engine caught fire after ingesting bird
274	28.04.52	T7	WA606	208 Sqdn	Egypt	Undershot on landing
275	28.04.52	F8	WA780	66 Sqdn	UK	Undercarriage collapsed on landing
276	29.04.52	F3	EE417	206 AFS	UK	*Crashed during low level aerobatics*
277	29.04.52	F4	RA480	205 AFS	UK	*Collided with VW298 at night in circuit*
278	29.04.52	F4	VW298	205 AFS	UK	*Collided with RA480 at night in circuit*
279	05.05.52	T7	VZ643	607 Sqdn	UK	*Pilot baled out unsuccessfully when lost*
280	05.05.52	FR9	WB119	79 Sqdn	Germ.	*Crashed during air to ground firing practice*
281	05.05.52	F8	WE929	64 Sqdn	UK	Collided with USAAF F86, pilot baled out
282	05.05.52	T7	WG992	206 AFS	UK	Undershot landing, hit windsock and railway
283	12.05.52	F4	VT145	215 AFS	UK	Undershot during single engine approach
284	13.05.52	F4	VT237	203 AFS	UK	Undershot during single engine approach
285	13.05.52	T7	WH167	207	UK	*Crashed at night, in circuit*

				AFS		
286	16.05.52	T7	WA679	RAFF C	UK	*Crashed during single engine overshoot (2)*
287	20.05.52	F4	VW274	203 AFS	UK	Landed with undercarriage unlocked at night
288	20.05.52	NF 11	WD607	141 Sqdn	UK	*Collided with another NF11 at night*
289	21.05.52	F4	VT176	203 AFS	UK	*Crashed soon after night take off*
290	21.05.52	F8	WF745	CGS	UK	*Dived into sea during attack on flag target*
291	28.05.52	PR 10	WB158	231 OCU	UK	*Crashed during single engine overshoot*
292	28.05.52	T7	WF854	65 Sqdn	UK	*Unexplained dive into ground from cloud (2)*
293	03.06.52	F8	WH292	54 Sqdn	UK	Undershot landing
294	04.06.52	FR9	WB120	208 Sqdn	Egypt	Stalled on landing, undercarriage collapsed
295	04.06.52	F8	WH399	500 Sqdn	France	Undercarriage collapsed on landing
296	06.06.52	F8	WK698	54 Sqdn	UK	Ran out of fuel, pilot baled out
297	06.06.52	F8	WK708	54 Sq	UK	Ran out of fuel, pilot baled out
298	06.06.52	F4	VT336	207 AFS	UK	*Unexplained dive into ground from cloud*
299	07.06.52	PR 10	WB161	13 Sqdn	Egypt	*Missing on flight to Cyprus*
300	09.06.52	F4	VT181	203 AFS	UK	Ran out of fuel, belly landed
301	16.06.52	T7	WL369	CFS	UK	Undershot landing
302	17.06.52	F4	VT344	203 AFS	UK	*Crashed soon after night take off*
303	17.06.52	FR9	VZ583	208 Sqdn	Egypt	Ran into slipstream, broke up, pilot baled out
304	20.06.52	F8	WA777	12Gp CF	UK	Collided with Wellington, pilot thrown out
305	21.06.52	T7	WA685	2 Sqdn	Belgm.	Undershot landing
306	24.06.52	F3	EE414	206 AFS	UK	*Broke up in air during aerobatics*

307	24.06.52	T7	WH229	215 AFS	UK	Undershot landing, caught fire
308	26.06.52	F4	RA486	RAFF C	UK	Take off abandoned, overshot runway
309	26.06.52	F8	WE861	226 OCU	UK	*Crashed during practice attack on another F8*
310	30.06.52	F3	EE465	206 AFS	UK	Engine flamed out on approach, belly landed
311	30.06.52	F4	RA483	2 FU	UK	Ran out of fuel on ferry flight, pilot baled out
312	08.07.52	F4	VT190	203 AFS	UK	Wheels collapsed on landing, caught fire
313	15.07.52	F4	RA 380	203 AFS	UK	Collided with Anson in circuit, crash landed
314	16.07.52	T7	WH130	203 AFS	UK	*Collided with an F4, pilots baled out (1)*
315	19.07.52	NF 11	WD716	228 OCU	UK	*Both engines put out, ditched in sea (2)*
316	22.07.52	F4	VT141	RAFF C	UK	Undershot landing, undercarriage collapsed
317	22.07.52	F4	VT264	215 AFS	UK	*Ran out of fuel, hit tree on approach*
318	22.07.52	FR9	WB139	79 Sqdn	Germ.	*Both engines failed, baled out unsuccessfully*
319	24.07.52	F4	RA369	215 AFS	UK	*Unexplained dive into sea*
320	24.07.52	NF 11	WD608	141 Sqdn	UK	*Dived into sea attacking towed target (2)*
321	24.07.52	F8	WA821	222 Sqdn	UK	*Flew into ground in bad visibility*
322	28.07.52	F8	WK647	54 Sqdn	UK	*Dived into ground*
323	31.07.52	F8	WA789	226 OCU	UK	Collided with another F8, pilot baled out
324	06.08.52	T7	WF828	226 OCU	UK	*Crashed on single engine overshoot (2)*
325	07.08.52	F8	WE947	1 Sqdn	UK	*Unexplained dive into ground from cloud*
326	07.08.52	T7	WF789	16 Sqdn	UK	Ran out of fuel, pilot baled out
327	07.08.52	T7	WF793	228	UK	*Flew into high ground in cloud*

				OCU		(2)
328	11.08.52	F4	RA376	215 AFS	UK	*Unexplained dive into ground from cloud*
329	13.08.52	F3	EE491	206 AFS	UK	*Unexplained dive into ground at night*
330	14.08.52	F8	WK657	92 Sqdn	UK	*Crashed during aerobatics*
331	19.08.52	F8	WA894	263 Sqdn	UK	Collided with another F8, pilot baled out
332	19.08.52	NF 11	WD714	228 OCU	UK	Collided with WD772, pilots baled out
333	19.08.52	NF 11	WD772	228 OCU	UK	*Collided with WD714 (2)*
334	20.08.52	F4	RA429	205 AFS	UK	*Dived into ground out of cloud*
335	20.08.52	T7	WA691	CFS	UK	Engine cut on single engine approach, hit wall
336	21.08.52	F8	VZ547	74 Sqdn	UK	Abandoned take off, overshot runway
337	01.09.52	NF 11	WD755	228 OCU	UK	Controls jammed on take off run, overshot
338	08.09.52	T7	WA621	226 OTU	UK	Undercarriage leg jammed up, crash landed
339	09.09.52	F4	EE401	206 AFS	UK	Collided with VZ405, pilot baled out
340	09.09.52	F4	VZ405	206 AFS	UK	Collided with EE401, pilot baled out
341	09.09.52	F8	VZ542	SF Tang.	UK	*Crashed during aerobatic practice*
342	09.09.52	F8	WA822	66 Sqdn	UK	*Unexplained dive into ground from cloud*
343	09.09.52	F8	WH294	226 OCU	UK	Ran out of fuel, ditched in English Channel
344	16.09.52	F4	VT127	203 AFS	UK	*Crashed during aerobatic practice (1 + 1 on ground)*
345	17.09.52	T7	WF883	1 OFU	Burma	Ran out of fuel, belly landed in field
346	17.09.52	T7	WL454	20 MU	UK	*Flew into ground after fly past (2)*
347	18.09.52	F8	WH276	616 Sqdn	UK	Overshot landing into rough ground

348	19.09.52	F4	VW294	215 AFS	UK	Undershot landing, undercarriage collapsed
349	21.09.52	NF 11	WD666	87 Sqdn	Germ.	Canopy misted up, crashed on overshoot
350	21.09.52	NF 11	WD685	87 Sqdn	Germ.	Canopy misted up, undershot runway
351	24.09.52	T7	WL409	266 Sqdn	Germ.	*Radio failed, flew into hill in cloud (2)*
352	26.09.52	F4	EE528	205 AFS	UK	*Spiralled into sea during aerobatic practice*
353	29.09.52	F8	WH472	263 Sqdn	UK	*Flew into hill in cloud after take off*
354	09.10.52	T7	WH217	CFS	UK	Stalled landing at night, wheels collapsed
355	10.10.52	NF 11	WD648	CFE	UK	Crashed back on ground after night take off
356	17.10.52	F8	WK749	72 Sqdn	UK	*Collided with WK690*
357	17.10.52	F8	WK690	72 Sqdn	UK	*Collided with WK749*
358	22.10.52	F4	VT224	215 AFS	UK	*Undershot on approach, cartwheeled*
359	22.10.52	F8	VZ563	63 Sqdn	UK	*Flew into ground while descending in cloud*
360	22.10.52	F8	VZ461	43 Sqdn	UK	*AH failed, dived into sea from cloud*
361	27.10.52	F4	VW268	205 AFS	UK	*Dived into ground at night from height*
362	04.11.52	F8	WF687	226 OCU	UK	Collided with WH362, belly landed at base
363	04.11.52	F8	WF362	226 OCU	UK	*Collided with WH687, lost wing*
364	06.11.52	F4	VT245	205 AFS	UK	Ran out of fuel in circuit, belly landed
365	06.11.52	T7	WF875	208 S	Egypt	Both engines cut, belly landed
366	07.11.52	T7	WF823	504 Sqdn	UK	*Canopy detached and jammed, crashed (2)*
367	07.11.52	T7	WL433	209 AFS	UK	*Stalled during asymmetric flying, crashed (2)*
368	17.11.52	NF 11	WD723	228 OCU	UK	*Seen smoking in shallow dive,*

						blew up (2)
369	17.11.52	F8	WE914	245 Sqdn	UK	*Stalled on single engine approach, crashed*
370	19.11.52	T7	WL372	203 AFS	UK	Stalled on approach, wheels collapsed
371	21.11.52	F4	VT341	215 AFS	UK	Ran out of fuel, crash landed in field
372	21.11.52	F4	VZ428	215 AFS	UK	*Flew into Humber mud flats and broke up*
373	25.11.52	T7	WG944	206 AFS	UK	*Stalled on approach, inverted, crashed*
374	02.12.52	F4	VT306	206 AFS	UK	Joystick jammed, overshot landing
375	02.12.52	NF 11	WD761	228 OCU	UK	Both engines cut at night, pilots baled out
376	04.12.52	T7	WL402	211 AFS	UK	*Crashed during asymmetric training (2)*
377	09.12.52	NF 11	WD757	228 OCU	UK	Undershot landing, finished wheels up
378	11.12.52	F8	WH455	616Sq	UK	*Collided with WH473 at night*
379	11.12.52	F8	WH473	616 Sqdn	UK	*Collided with WH455 at night*
380	12.12.52	T7	WF774	66 Sqdn	UK	*Rolled, crashed after take off (2)*
381	12.12.52	T7	WH234	205 AFS	UK	*Crashed soon after night take off (2)*
382	12.12.52	F8	WH425	CGS	UK	Stalled on first landing, belly landed 2nd time
383	18.12.52	F4	VT218	206AFS	UK	Collided with WG978, baled out
384	18.12.52	F8	WG978	206 AFS	UK	*Collided with VT218, crashed*
385	18.12.52	FR9	VW365	2 Sqdn	Germ	*Rolled and dived into ground in circuit*
386	18.12.52	F8	WH424	247 Sqdn	UK	Collided with WH442, landed safely
387	18.12.52	F8	WH442	247 Sqdn	UK	*Collided with WH424, pilot tried to bale out*
388	22.12.52	PR10	WB173	541 S	Germ	Wheels selected up on landing
399	22.12.52	F8	WK651	54 Sqdn	UK	Flew into wood on attempted overshoot
400	31.12.52	T7	WF852	CFS	UK	*Unexplained dive into ground*

						from cloud

163 write-offs and 93 deaths in 1952

In 1952 alone a Meteor was lost nearly every 2 days and a life lost every 4 days. By the end of 1952, 400 Meteors were lost by the RAF/RAuxAF through accident, with 226 fatalities of which 39 could be attributed to unexplained diving into the ground.

401	02.01.53	T7	WL365	205 AFS	UK	*Unexplained dive into ground from cloud*
402	19.01.53	T7	WA715	205 AFS	UK	Overstressed in flight
403	21.01.53	NF 11	WD654	264 Sqdn	UK	Ran out of fuel in bad visibility, baled out
404	26.01.53	T7	WL432	209 AFS	UK	Undershot landing
405	28.01.53	NF 11	WM169	96 Sqdn	Neth.	Ran out of fuel in bad visibility, baled out
406	29.01.53	FR9	VZ580	2 Sqdn	Germ.	Running short of fuel, belly landed in field
407	02.02.53	F4	VT265	209 AFS	UK	*Dived into ground in sleet shower*
408	02.02.52	F4	VW282	203 AFS	UK	*Missing on aerobatic exercise*
409	04.02.53	F8	WK924	211 AFS	UK	*Unexplained dive into ground from cloud*
410	05.02.52	FR9	VW368	208 Sqdn	Egypt	Structural failure, pilot baled out
411	05.02.52	F8	WE957	41 Sqdn	UK	Struck by towed flag, overshot forced landing
412	07.02.53	F8	WH513	500Sq	UK	Overshot landing, hit trees
413	09.02.53	T7	WA608	208 AFS	UK	Collided with F4 on take off, crash landed
414	09.02.53	T7	WL455	209 AFS	UK	*Dived into ground out of cloud (2)*
415	11.02.53	PR 10	VS983	541 Sqdn	UK	*Crashed on single engine approach*
416	13.02.53	F4	VT321	215 AFS	UK	Both engines cut, hit trees on forced landing
417	17.02.53	FR9	VB142	79 Sqdn	Germ.	Flew into trees on overshoot (bad weather)
418	18.02.53	F4	VT133	215	UK	Undershot landing, undercarriage

112

				AFS		collapsed
419	22.02.53	F8	WA839	43 Sqdn	UK	*Unexplained dive into ground at night*
420	25.02.53	F8	WH311	226Sq	OCU	*Pilot baled out unsuccessfully*
421	25.02.53	T7	WL381	CFS	UK	*Spun into ground after slow roll (2)*
422	27.02.53	F8	WH477	257 Sqdn	UK	Flew into target flag, pilot baled out
423	11.03.53	F4	VT304	209 AFS	UK	*Unexplained dive into sea at night*
424	11.03.53	NF 11	WD770	141 Sqdn	UK	Landed wheels up in error
425	14.03.53	F8	WA762	CGS	UK	Flew into ground on approach (bad weather)
426	15.03.53	F4	RA448	215 AFS	UK	Collided with VW262, belly landed
427	15.03.53	F4	VW262	215 AFS	UK	Collided with RA448, pilot baled out
428	17.03.53	F4	VT169	203 AFS	UK	Undercarriage collapsed on landing
429	18.03.53	F8	WH351	19 Sqdn	UK	*Collided with WK858 in formation*
430	18.03.53	F8	WK858	19 Sqdn	UK	*Collided with WH351 in formation*
431	19.03.53	NF 11	WD676	68 Sqdn	Neth.	*Pilot suffered anoxia, one baled out*
432	24.03.53	F8	WH358	DFLS	UK	*Missing*
433	25.03.53	F8	WA809	DFLS	UK	Aileron malfunction, overshot landing
434	26.03.53	NF 11	WD789	87 Sqdn	Germ.	Runway blocked, hit vehicle when landing
435	27.03.53	F8	WE956	41 Sqdn	Belg.	Both engines cut, wheels collapsed on landing
436	29.03.53	F8	WF760	615 Sqdn	UK	*Control lost in cloud, dived into ground*
437	30.03.53	NF 11	WD713	228 OCU	UK	Tyre burst on take off, belly landed
438	04.04.53	FR9	WB117	208 Sqdn	Qatar	Ran out of fuel, belly landed in desert
439	07.04.53	T7	WG972	231 OCU	UK	*Overshooting at night, crashed*

440	08.04.53	T7	WF857	202 AFS	UK	Crashed on approach trying to miss other plane
441	08.04.53	T7	WH230	SF Bens.	UK	Stalled on approach, crashed
442	08.04.53	T7	VT240	203AFS	UK	Hit by other plane during landing
443	13.04.53	F8	WH347	CGS	UK	*Lost aileron tab, wing broke off, crashed*
444	17.04.53	F8	VZ501	72 Sqdn	UK	*Unexplained dive into sea from cloud*
445	17.04.53	T7	WG988	209 AFS	UK	Lost power on take off, overshot runway
446	20.04.53	T7	WG989	206 AFS	UK	*Air brakes left out, rolled in circuit, crashed*
447	25.04.53	F8	WF747	600 Sqdn	UK	*Lost hood, attempted bale out failed*
448	04.05.53	T7	WH246	205 AFS	UK	*Hit radio mast on low level run, crashed (2)*
449	05.05.53	F8	VZ446	74 Sqdn	UK	*Hit ground during practice ground attack*
450	10.05.53	T7	WA595	605 Sqdn	UK	Both engines cut, undershot belly landing
451	13.05.53	T7	WL431	39 Sqdn	Egypt	*Rolled after dummy attack and crashed*
452	15.05.53	T7	WF821	64 Sqdn	UK	*Unexplained crash into North Sea (2)*
453	19.05.53	F8	WK929	211 AFS	UK	*Dived into ground from cloud after take off*
454	28.05.53	F8	VZ481	257 Sqdn	UK	Pilot baled out from spin
455	09.06.53	F8	WK823	211 AFS	UK	Stalled on landing, undercarriage collapsed
456	10.06.53	T7	WL362	203 AFS	UK	Pilots baled out from spin
457	13.06.53	NF 11	WM 258	264 Sqdn	UK	*Flew into high ground in cloud*
458	17.06.53	T7	WG971	206 AFS	UK	*Flew into ground at night*
459	18.06.53	F4	VT266	209 AFS	UK	Engines failed on take off run, ran into field
460	19.06.53	T7	VW483	215 AFS	UK	*Crashed during single engine practice (2)*

461	24.06.53	F4	VZ412	203 AFS	UK	Pilot baled out after losing control
462	29.06.53	T7	WF779	500 Sqdn	UK	*Crashed during single engine practice approach (2)*
463	03.07.53	F8	WE862	616 Sqdn	UK	*Dived into sea, dinghy inflated accidentally?*
464	08.07.53	F8	VZ556	257 Sqdn	UK	*Collided with VZ560, tried to bale out unsuccessfully*
465	08.07.53	F8	VZ560	257 Sqdn	UK	*Collided with VZ556, crashed*
466	08.07.53	T7	WA735	SF Leuch	UK	*Hood opened after take off, crashed*
467	10.07.53	T7	VW445	209 AFS	UK	During single engine practice, belly landed in error
468	14.07.53	T7	WL397	211 AFS	UK	Stalled on approach, undershot landing
469	16.07.53	FR9	WX973	79 Sqdn	Germ.	*Hit tree on approach, cartwheeled*
470	17.07.53	T7	WH243	264 Sqdn	UK	Undershot single engine approach, caught fire
471	17.07.53	NF 11	WM 166	228 OCU	UK	Undershot landing, undercarriage collapsed
472	20.07.53	F8	WK724	Nth. Sect.	Malta	Brakes failed, overshot landing, hit wall
473	21.07.53	F4	VT138	215 AFS	UK	*Flew into ground in cloud*
474	22.07.53	F8	WK978	64 Sqdn	UK	*Unexplained dive into ground from cloud*
475	24.07.53	FR9	WB113	79 Sqdn	Neth.	*Ran out of fuel, pilot tried to bale out*
476	27.07.53	F8	WK917	1 Sqdn	UK	Damaged by engine blade failure
477	28.07.53	NF 11	WM 222	68 Sqdn	Belgm.	*Flew into trees at night (2)*
478	29.07.53	NF 11	WM 146	256 Sqdn	Germ.	*Collided with F86, pilot baled out unsuccessfully*
479	07.08.53	T7	WA596	249 Sqdn	Egypt	Swung on landing, undercarriage collapsed
480	10.08.53	F4	VZ406	206 AFS	UK	Abandoned in spin during aerobatic practice
481	10.08.53	T7	WA724	141	UK	*Flew into approach lights*

				Sqdn		*during night landing*
482	15.08.53	NF 11	WM 226	AWDS	UK	Take off abandoned, overshot runway, caught fire
483	16.08.53	F8	WA856	1 Sqdn	Frnce	*Collided with WA868*
484	16.08.53	F8	WA868	1 Sqdn	Frnce	*Collided with WA856*
485	17.08.53	F4	VT290	JCU	UK	*Hit ground attempting recovery from dive, anoxia?*
486	18.08.53	F8	WA758	19 Sqdn	UK	*Hit ground during low flying exercise*
487	18.08.53	F8	WE879	CGS	UK	Lost leading edge of wing, belly landed at high speed
488	18.08.53	F8	WE951	56 Sqdn	UK	Abandoned take off, overshot through fence into field
489	18.08.53	F8	WE964	66 Sq	UK	*Tail broke off in flight*
490	19.08.53	NF 11	WM177	85 Sqdn	UK	*Dived into ground in night interception exercise (2)*
491	21.08.53	NF 11	WD659	87 Sqdn	Germ.	Apparent loss of power after take off, crash landed
492	21.08.53	T7	WG967	60Sq	Sing.	Wheels jammed up, belly landed
493	22.08.53	F8	WA933	222 Sqdn	UK	*Flew into house descending out of cloud*
494	23.08.53	F8	WK966	64 Sqdn	UK	Hit slipstream on approach, crash landed
495	31.08.53	T7	WH189	87 Sqdn	Germ.	*Hit wires during low level practice interception (2)*
496	02.09.53	F8	WE917	211 AFS	UK	*Lost leading edge of wing, inverted, dived into ground*
497	03.09.53	F4	RA475	206 AFS	UK	*Unexplained dive into ground*
498	04.09.53	F8	WA778	66 Sqdn	UK	*Broke up recovering from dive*
499	04.09.53	F8	WF648	257 Sqdn	UK	*Broke up in air*
500	08.09.53	T7	WA712	209 AFS	UK	*Overstressed and broke up in air*
501	08.09.53	NF 11	WD621	256 Sqdn	Germ.	Caught fire in air, pilots baled out
502	11.09.53	NF 11	WD788	96 Sqdn	Germ.	Hit trees on approach in bad weather, crash landed

503	11.09.53	F8	WF695	SF Horsh	UK	*Hit by Meteor in BofB practice, lost tail and crashed*
504	19.09.53	F8	WA836	74 Sqdn	UK	*Broke up in low level roll in Battle of Britain display*
505	19.09.53	F8	WA927	56 Sqdn	UK	*Broke up in low level roll in Battle of Britain display*
506	21.09.53	NF 13	WM324	219 Sqdn	Germ.	Sank back on take off, u/c collapsed, caught fire
507	25.09.53	T7	WF792	67 Sqdn	Germ.	*Rolled and crashed during single engine overshoot (2)*
508	27.09.53	F8	WE912	616 Sqdn	UK	*Engine caught fire in air, pilot baled out unsuccessfully*
509	28.09.53	F8	WH407	226 OCU	UK	*Hit ground after practice attack on other Meteor*
510	30.09.53	F8	WH407	226 OCU	UK	*Hit ground recovering from dive*
511	02.10.53	F8	WE856	19 Sqdn	UK	*Broke up in air after aerobatics*
512	05.10.53	F8	WK939	222 Sqdn	UK	Caught fire during air to ground firing, pilot baled out
513	14.10.53	F3	EE462	210 AFS	UK	*Lost control in cloud, hit ground recovering from dive*
514	14.10.53	F4	VT303	209 AFS	UK	*Pilot baled out during inverted spin, not found*
515	20.10.53	NF 11	WD603	29 Sqdn	UK	Ran out of fuel on approach, ditched
516	26.10.53	F8	WH467	263 Sqdn	UK	*Lost hood during practice attack on B-29, hit ground*
517	29.10.53	F4	VT335	206 AFS	UK	Heavy landing, undercarriage collapsed
518	31.10.53	FR9	WB118	79 Sqdn	Germ.	*Flew into hill in cloud during low level exercise*
519	02.11.53	F4	VT305	209 AFS	UK	Undershot runway on night landing
520	03.11.53	F4	VT293	206 AFS	UK	Heavy landing, wheels collapsed, ventral tank caught fire
521	04.11.53	F8	WK886	245Sq	UK	*Hit target cable? Crashed*
522	07.11.53	F8	WF640	500 Sqdn	UK	Collided with WK805 during practice attack, pilot baled out
523	07.11.53	F8	WF805	500	UK	*Collided with WF640 during*

				Sqdn		*practice attack, crashed*
524	09.11.53	T7	WL458	CFS	UK	*During asymmetric training inverted and hit trees (2)*
525	10.11.53	T7	WH131	CFS	UK	Baled out during inverted spin
526	13.11.53	F8	WE882	CGS	UK	Stalled on final approach, undershot, crash landed
527	14.11.53	F8	WH383	610 Sqdn	UK	*Flew into hill in cloud in formation*
528	14.11.53	F8	WH384	610 Sqdn	UK	*Flew into hill in cloud in formation*
529	17.11.53	F8	WA854	1 Sqdn	UK	Collided with target
530	21.11.53	F8	WA967	253 Sqdn	UK	Engine caught fire in air
531	25.11.53	F8	WA779	66 Sqdn	UK	Heavy landing, undercarriage collapsed
532	30.11.53	FR9	VZ594	208 Sqdn	Egypt	*Lost control, pilot baled out unsuccessfully*
533	30.11.53	F8	WA835	226 OCU	UK	Collided with Meteor WE872, pilot baled out
534	03.12.53	F4	VW261	215 AFS	UK	Undershot landing on single engine approach, caught fire
535	03.12.53	T7	WG982	206 AFS	UK	Crashed during single engine approach
536	14.12.53	F8	WL119	263 Sqdn	UK	Undershot landing at night
537	16.12.53	F8	WA769	56 Sqdn	UK	Ran out of fuel in bad weather, pilot baled out
538	16.12.53	F8	WA930	56 Sqdn	UK	Ran out of fuel in bad weather, pilot baled out
539	16.12.53	F8	WH283	56 Sqdn	UK	Ran out of fuel in bad weather, pilot baled out
540	16.12.53	F8	WH510	56 Sqdn	UK	Ran out of fuel in bad weather, force landed
541	17.12.53	T7	WH116	13 Sqdn	Egypt	Both engines failed, undershot belly landing
542	29.12.53	T7	WH197	215 AFS	UK	*Crashed on approach, cartwheeled and blew up*
543	31.12.53	F4	RA427	215 AFS	UK	Undershot single engine landing, undercarriage torn off
544	31.12.53	T7	WA654	RAFF	UK	*Engine caught fire, pilot baled*

				C		out unsuccessfully

144 write-offs and 83 deaths in 1953

545	11.01.54	NF 11	WM23 3	68 Sqdn	Germ	Ran out of fuel in bad weather, belly landed in field
546	18.01.54	T7	WH220	78 Wing	Malta	Crashed on take off
547	19.01.54	T7	WA632	207 AFS	UK	*Hit tree and rolled into ground in circuit*
548	19.01.54	F8	WH288	226 OCU	UK	*Dived into sea out of cloud during firing practice*
549	21.01.54	NF 11	WM17 5	85 Sqdn	UK	*Ran out of fuel in bad weather, unsuccessful bale out*
550	24.01.54	F8	WH298	257 Sqdn	UK	*Crashed during display practice, structural failure?*
551	26.01.54	T7	VZ629	66 Sqdn	UK	Short of fuel, force landed, undercarriage torn off
552	08.02.54	NF 11	WM25 1	151 Sqdn	UK	Take off, tyre burst, wheels collapsed, wing tank caught fire
553	12.02.54	F4	VT313	209 AFS	UK	Landed wheels up accidentally
554	12.02.54	T7	VW430	209 AFS	UK	*Flew into ground in circuit in bad weather at night*
555	12.02.54	T7	VW244	209 AFS	UK	*Flew into ground in bad weather at night*
556	13.02.54	F8	WF754	600 Sqdn	UK	*Lost hood and dived into ground*
557	16.02.54	T7	WL430	26 Sqdn	Germ .	Yawed on take off, wing tip hit ground, cartwheeled
558	20.02.54	F8	WK692	604 Sqdn	UK	*Collided with WK696, spiralled into ground*
559	20.02.54	F8	WK696	604 Sqdn	UK	*Collided with WK692, dived into ground*
560	24.02.54	FR9	VZ600	79 Sqdn	Germ .	Hit birds and engine caught fire, belly landed on grass
561	01.03.54	T7	WF815	207 AFS	UK	*Abandoned in spin after slow roll*
562	05.03.54	F8	WK863	245 Sqdn	UK	*Collided with WK891 during practice attack on Sabres*
563	05.03.54	F8	WK891	245	UK	Collided with WK863, returned

				Sqdn		to base OK
564	11.03.54	F8	WH478	56 Sqdn	UK	Nose wheel fell off during take off, belly landed on return
565	12.03.54	T7	WL423	209 AFS	UK	*Missing on training flight, presumed ditched (2)*
566	17.03.54	F4	VT309	209 AFS	UK	Abandoned take off, wheels raised to stop, caught fire
567	18.03.54	NF 11	VM248	87 Sqdn	Germ.	*Flew into ground out of cloud in bad weather*
568	24.03.54	NF 11	WD778	228 OCU	UK	*Flew into high ground on approach to landing (2)*
569	26.03.54	F4	VT171	209 AFS	UK	Hit slipstream of previous aircraft on approach, undershot
570	26.03.54	T7	WA734	605 Sqdn	UK	Swung on take off, wheels raised to stop, caught fire
571	31.03.54	F8	WH312	ETPS	UK	*Engine failed on approach, crashed*
572	03.04.54	F8	WL128	111 Sqdn	UK	Collided with WL462, pilot baled out
573	03.04.54	T7	WL462	604 Sqdn	UK	*Collided with WL128, pilot baled out unsuccessfully*
574	08.04.54	FR9	VZ582	208 Sqdn	Tunisia	Ran out of fuel, belly landed in bad visibility
575	08.04.54	FR9	WH538	208 Sqdn	Tunisia	Ran out of fuel, belly landed in bad visibility
576	08.04.54	FR9	WB143	2 Sqdn	Germ.	*Hit cable and crashed*
577	11.04.54	T7	WF850	611 Sqdn	UK	Hit pond during single engine force landing
578	12.04.54	F4	EE525	207 AFS	UK	*Aircraft dived into ground, pilot baled out, lost at sea*
579	26.04.54	NF 14	WS746	85 Sqdn	UK	*Short of fuel at night over sea, bale out failed*
580	27.04.54	F4	VT194	207 AFS	UK	Damaged in heavy landing
581	30.04.54	T7	WF837	612 Sqdn	UK	Iced up, bounced on emergency landing and cartwheeled
582	30.04.54	NF 13	WM321	219 Sqdn	Egypt	Engine caught fire
583	13.05.54	F4	RA419	209 AFS	UK	Undercarriage damaged in heavy landing

584	22.05.54	F8	WH278	616 Sqdn	UK	*Dived into ground out of cloud, electrical failure?*
585	27.05.54	F8	WH422	226 OCU	UK	*Hood disintegrated, crashed*
586	27.05.54	NF 11	WM240	87 Sqdn	Germ.	Engine cowling opened during take off, crashed, caught fire
587	28.05.54	F4	EE590	207 AFS	UK	Sank back on ground after take off, damaged undercarriage

This is when I left 616 Squadron and transferred to 501 County of Gloucester Squadron in Bristol. During my otherwise enjoyable 3 years with 616 Squadron many 616 pilots were killed due to accident.

588	03.06.54	F8	WH308	226 OCU	UK	*Lost control at low altitude, crashed*
589	03.06.54	T7	WL483	8 FTS	UK	Abandoned in spin
590	08.06.54	F8	WK906	211 FTS	UK	*Hit ground during low level exercise in bad visibility*
591	10.06.54	PR 10	VS972	541 Sqdn	Medit.	Collided with VS973, crash landed at Istres
592	10.06.54	PR10	VS973	541S	Medit	Collided with VS972, baled out
593	11.06.54	F4	VT183	8 FTS	UK	Swung on take off, undercarriage raised to stop
594	14.06.54	F8	WK722	601 Sqdn	Malta	Nose wheel fell off during take off, belly landed on return
595	21.06.54	F4	RA436	12 FTS	UK	Lost leading edge during aerobatics, belly landed
596	24.06.54	F8	VZ470	226 OCU	UK	Undershot, undercarriage collapsed, belly tank caught fire
597	28.06.54	T7	WH239	228 OCU	UK	*Lost hood after take off, abandoned aircraft*
598	29.06.54	NF 12	WS600	85 Sqdn	UK	*Both engs. cut, tried to abandon, dived into ground (2)*
599	30.06.54	F4	RA428	8 FTS	UK	Wheels jammed, belly landed
600	07.07.54	F4	VT195	4 FTS	UK	Undercarriage collapsed on landing
601	15.07.54	F8	WA852	257 S	UK	Hood shattered, ejected
602	18.07.54	F8	WB107	19 Sqdn	UK	Overshot runway during braking test
603	18.07.54	F8	WL132	604 Sqdn	UK	Overshot abandoned take-off, wheels retracted to stop
604	24.07.54	F8	WE897	43	UK	*Collided with WL114 during*

				Sqdn		*interception exercise*
605	24.07.54	F8	WL114	43 Sqdn	UK	Collided with WE897, ejected
606	27.07.54	NF 11	WM18 4	527 Sqdn	Germ .	Ran out of fuel, force landed
607	28.07.54	T7	WL374	CFS	UK	*Hit WL457, lost tail (2)*
608	28.07.54	T7	WL457	CFS	UK	*Collided with WL374, spun into ground (2)*
609	03.08.54	F4	VT231	4 FTS	UK	Engine cut on roller landing, yawed, wheels collapsed
610	09.08.54	F4	VT109	4 FTS	UK	Nose wheel collapsed while stationary before take off
611	09.08.54	F8	WK936	245 Sqdn	UK	*Hit hangar during practice ground attack*
612	16.08.54	F8	WA966	DFLS	UK	*Dived into ground out of cloud*
613	27.08.54	T7	WH190	8 FTS	UK	*Uncontrolled dive, baled out unsuccessfully*
614	27.08.54	F8	WH458	RAF FC	UK	*Dived into ground out of cloud*
615	31.08.54	F4	VT285	12 FTS	UK	Sank onto runway during overshoot
616	03.09.54	F8	WF714	500 Sqdn	Malta	Undershot runway on landing, wheels collapsed
617	09.09.54	F8	WA983	64 Sqdn	UK	Collided with WF764 during exercise, baled out
618	09.09.54	F8	WF764	64 Sqdn	UK	Collided with WA983 during exercise, baled out
619	10.09.54	FR9	VZ588	208 Sqdn	Egypt	Lost wheel on take off, landed, caught fire
620	11.09.54	T7	WL343	4 FTS	UK	*Crashed after low level slow roll during display practice*
621	13.09.54	F8	WH287	263 Sqdn	UK	*Broke up in turn*
622	18.09.54	F8	WH302	610 Sqdn	UK	*Crashed doing aerobatics in display*
623	19.09.54	F8	WK826	211 FTS	UK	Abandoned after losing hood on take off, hit hut
624	20.09.54	F4	RA365	8 FTS	UK	*Lost engine, rolled into ground on landing approach*
625	21.09.54	NF 11	WD593	151 Sqdn	UK	Collided with WD643 during landing

626	26.09.54	T7	WG973	SF Brug.	Germ.	*Rolled on overshoot, crashed*
627	03.10.54	T7	WA629	602Sq	UK	Baled out after instrument failure
628	04.10.54	F8	VZ522	226 OCU	UK	Collided with WH400, baled out
629	04.10.54	F8	VH400	226 OCU	UK	Collided with VZ522, baled out
630	04.10.54	NF 12	WS691	152 Sqdn	UK	*Hit by F-86 of the USAF, crashed on approach (2)*
631	06.10.54	F8	WH314	64 Sqdn	UK	**Swung on take off, undercarriage collapsed, caught fire**
632	13.10.54	PR 10	VS969	81 Sqdn	Sing.	Struck water and sea wall on approach, crashed on runway
633	15.10.54	F8	WK679	72 Sqdn	UK	*Inverted and dived into ground on apparent overshoot*
634	19.10.54	F8	WL139	64 Sqdn	UK	Hit ground during formation aerobatics, crash landed
635	21.10.54	NF 11	WM 179	87 Sqdn	Germ.	*Flew into ground during GCA approach in cloud (2)*
636	26.10.54	F4	RA489	8 FTS	UK	Nose wheel raised in error after landing
637	26.10.54	T7	WL418	4 FTS	UK	Lost power on approach, hit railway embankment
638	28.10.54	F8	WH444	SF Odi.	UK	Undercarriage retracted in error on landing, caught fire
639	30.10.54	T7	WH225	607 Sqdn	UK	Yawed on overshoot, wing hit ground, crashed
640	01.11.54	NF 11	WM188	141 Sqdn	Germ.	Hit slipstream on approach and crashed
641	04.11.54	F8	WA773	245 Sqdn	UK	Undercarriage collapsed on landing
642	15.11.54	F4	VT232	4 FTS	UK	*Lost power after take off at night and crashed*
643	17.11.54	FR9	VZ611	2 Sqdn	Germ.	Hit trees on approach and crashed short of runway
644	18.11.54	F8	WE938	63 Sqdn	UK	Collided with banner target during air to air firing exercise
645	19.11.54	F4	VW302	12 FTS	UK	*Instruments failed, ran out of fuel, tried to bale out*
646	25.11.54	F8	WA922	56 Sq	UK	Overshot landing

647	01.12.54	T7	WL467	12 FTS	UK	Engine failed on single engine overshoot, crash landed
648	02.12.54	F8	WK920	211 FTS	UK	Undercarriage damage in roller landing
649	03.12.54	F8	WA999	56 Sqdn	UK	Undercarriage failed to lower, belly landed
650	03.12.54	FR9	WX974	2 Sqdn.	Germ	*Dived into ground during combat practice*
651	05.12.54	F8	WH408	604 Sqdn	UK	Spun during practice interception, baled out
652	09.12.54	T7	WL363	IofAM	Germ	*Dived into ground out of cloud*
653	10.12.54	F4	VT215	8 FTS	UK	Turbine disc sheared off damaging airframe
654	14.12.54	T7	VW450	SF Dux.	UK	Ran short of fuel in bad weather, baled out
655	15.12.54	T7	VW419	8 FTS	UK	*Hit trees after night take off and broke up (2)*
656	18.12.54	T7	WL404	208 Sqdn	Libya	Ran out of fuel and crash landed on road
657	21.12.54	F8	WB108	211 FTS	UK	*Flew into ground out of cloud*
658	21.12.54	F8	WH299	263 Sqdn	UK	Abandoned in spin
659	21.12.54	F8	WK723	CGS	UK	*Dived into ground out of cloud*

115 write-offs and 54 deaths in 1954

660	05.01.55	F8	WA788	RAE	UK	Damaged on landing
661	10.01.55	T7	WA666	12 FTS	UK	*Dived into ground after take off (2)*
662	10.01.55	T7	WL342	FTU	UK	*Dived into ground after take off*
663	11.01.55	T7	WF783	72 Sqdn	UK	*Yawed on overshoot (single engine?) and crashed (2)*
664	25.01.55	NF 12	WS670	46 Sqdn	UK	Undercarriage collapsed on heavy landing
665	25.01.55	NF 14	WS835	46 Sqdn	UK	Ran out of fuel at night, baled out
666	01.02.55	F4	VT115	4 FTS	UK	*Side-slipped into ground in circuit at night*
667	01.02.55	T7	WF849	ITF Nic.	Cyprus	*Stalled after take off and crashed*

668	02.02.55	T7	WL408	12 FTS	UK	*Stalled and crashed on low level exercise (2)*
669	15.02.55	T7	WH194	12 FTS	UK	Baled out in spin during aerobatic exercise
670	22.02.55	NF 11	WM169	87 Sqdn	Germ	*Stalled on approach after fire warning, crashed (2)*
671	26.02.55	F8	WE884	63 Sqdn	UK	Hit birds, engine caught fire, baled out
672	03.03.55	F8	WE963	34 Sqdn	UK	*Collided with Fleet Air Arm Vampire*
673	07.03.55	T7	WL461	211 FTS	UK	Hit trees on night approach in snow, crash landed
674	09.03.55	T7	WH200	CFS	UK	*Spun into ground during single engine practice (2)*
675	16.03.55	T7	WL354	211 AFS	UK	*Dived into ground during aerobatics (2)*
676	20.03.55	T7	WA670	604 Sqdn	UK	Lost hood, baled out
677	23.03.55	NF 11	WD650	228 OCU	UK	*Crashed soon after abandoning night approach (2)*
678	01.04.55	T7	WL474	211 FTS	UK	*Crashed during single engine overshoot (2)*
679	13.04.55	F8	WK755	FCCS	UK	Overshot landing, swung and undercarriage collapsed
680	14.04.55	F4	VT235	8 FTS	UK	Landed with wheels up in error
681	15.04.55	T7	WL355	79 Sqdn	Neth.	Both engines cut due to error, landed wheels up
682	19.04.55	F8	WH378	56 Sq	UK	Collided with WK726, baled out
683	19.04.55	F8	WK726	56 Sqdn	UK	Collided with WH378, baled out
684	21.04.55	NF 11	WD754	256 Sqdn	Germ	*Blinded by searchlights soon after take off, crashed (2)*
685	21.04.55	T7	WL364	CFS	UK	Undershot landing and collapsed undercarriage
686	26.04.55	F4	VT328	8 FTS	UK	Overshot landing, undercarriage collapsed
687	28.04.55	F4	VZ392	12 FTS	UK	Bounced off ground
688	09.05.55	NF 11	WM268	141 Sqdn	UK	*Crashed in sea on night interception exercise (2)*
689	10.05.55	F8	WA819	63	UK	*Control lost in cloud,*

				Sqdn		*attempted bale out*
690	12.05.55	F8	WE904	211 FTS	UK	*Dived out of cloud, hit ground on attempted recovery*
691	20.05.55	NF 11	WD605	29 Sqdn	UK	*Crashed into sea during air to air firing exercise (2)*
692	26.05.55	F8	WE916	211 FTS	UK	*Dived into ground at night*
693	10.06.55	F8	WK933	26 APC	Cyprus	Lost canopy, airframe damaged
694	13.06.55	F4	RA425	8 FTS	UK	Wheels locked, belly landed
695	15.06.55	F4	VT263	8 FTS	UK	*Dived into ground from high altitude*
696	24.06.55	FR9	WL265	79 Sqdn	Germ.	*Hit obstruction, attempted bale out*
697	30.06.55	NF 12	WS662	153 Sqdn	UK	*Failed to get airborne on take off, ran into farm (2+2)*
698	07.07.55	F8	WA891	63 Sq	UK	*Dived into ground out of cloud*
699	07.07.55	F8	WL178	72 Sqdn	UK	Abandoned take off, undercarriage raised to stop
700	19.07.55	F8	WH348	19 Sqdn	UK	Tyre burst on landing, skidded into wall
701	05.08.55	PR 10	VS986	81 Sqdn	Sing.	Abandoned take off, undercarriage raised to stop
702	08.08.55	F8	WH379	45 Sqdn	Malay.	Undershot runway
703	09.08.55	F8	WL158	54 Sqdn	UK	Undercarriage collapsed on landing
704	15.08.55	F8	WH395	FWS	UK	*Collided with WK982*
705	15.08.55	F8	WK982	FWS	UK	*Collided with WH395*
706	16.08.55	NF 11	WD632	256 Sqdn	Germ.	Engine cut on take off, crash landed
707	17.08.55	F8	VZ549	613 Sqdn	Gibr.	Hit sea on approach, crash landed on runway
708	18.08.55	F8	WK732	FWS	UK	Overstressed after pilot suffered anoxia
709	27.08.55	F8	WH249	19 Sq	UK	*Flew into high ground in cloud*
710	05.09.55	FR9	WB122	79 Sqdn	Neth.	*Engine lost power on approach, crashed*
711	14.09.55	F8	WH375	APS Sylt	Germ.	Undercarriage damaged in heavy landing
712	15.09.55	F8	WK820	245Sq	UK	*Hit ground during loop*

713	21.09.55	FR 10	WB169	81 Sqdn	Sing.	Lost hydraulic pressure, belly landed
714	21.09.55	NF 12	WS621	AWO CU	UK	*Hit by WS683, baled out unsuccessfully*
715	21.09.55	NF 12	WS683	AWO CU	UK	*Collided with WS621, baled out unsuccessfully*
716	23.09.55	FR9	WL262	79 Sqdn	Germ.	Engine caught fire, undercarriage jammed, belly landed
717	26.09.55	NF 11	WD682	68 Sqdn	Germ.	Collided with target WH236, baled out
718	26.09.55	T7	WD236	68 Sqdn	Germ.	Collided with WH682, baled out
719	16.10.55	T7	WH115	605 Sqdn	UK	Brakes failed on landing, ran into ditch
720	04.11.55	T7	WG947	231 OCU	UK	*Engine lost power on take off, rolled into ground*
721	11.11.55	F8	WH377	APS Sylt	Germ.	Ventral tank caught fire during take off, landed safely
722	19.11.55	F8	WH253	600 Sqdn	UK	Stalled on approach, crash landed
723	21.11.55	F8	WL133	19 Sqdn	UK	Brakes failed while taxying, hit hangar
724	29.11.55	F8	WL141	65 Sqdn	UK	Undercarriage collapsed on landing
725	30.12.55	T7	VW449	FTU	UK	Lost hydraulic pressure, belly landed
726	30.12.55	NF 14	WS732	25 Sqdn	UK	Tyre burst on take off, caught fire

66 write-offs and 44 deaths in 1955

727	01.01.56	F8	WE873	504 Sqdn	UK	Baled out in spin
728	09.01.56	NF 14	WS727	153 Sqdn	UK	*Lost control in aerobatic roll, crashed (2)*
729	10.01.56	F8	WH443	25 Sqdn	UK	Undercarriage jammed, belly landed
730	11.01.56	NF 12	WS619	AWO CU	UK	Hit tree on approach at night
731	20.01.56	NF 12	WS661	AWO CU	UK	*Hit houses while low flying (2+2 on ground)*
732	24.01.56	NF	WS784	CFE	UK	Ran out of fuel in bad weather,

		14				baled out
733	22.02.56	F8	VZ507	APS Sylt	Germ.	Undercarriage retracted in error while taxying
734	15.03.56	PR9	WH542	2 Sqdn	Germ.	Collided with WB124 on approach, crash landed
735	17.03.56	F8	WK808	1 Sqdn	UK	Undercarriage collapsed on landing
736	03.04.56	PR 10	WB176	13 Sqdn	Cyprus	Collided with WH569, baled out
737	03.04.56	PR 10	WH569	13 Sqdn	Cyprus	Collided with WB176, belly landed
738	16.04.56	NF 12	WS694	153 Sqdn	UK	*Flew into ground after take off at night (2)*
739	19.04.56	F8	WH466	43 Sq	UK	Hit runway on overshoot
740	22.04.56	F8	WE895	609 Sqdn	UK	*Lost control in dive, baled out unsuccessfully*
741	11.05.56	PR9	WB124	2 Sqn	Germ	Pilot blacked out, stressed a/c
742	14.05.56	F8	WH415	63 Sqdn	UK	Undershot landing damaging undercarriage
743	17.05.56	NF 13	WS831	264 Sqdn	UK	Brakes failed on landing, hit building
744	28.05.56	NF 11	WD734	68 Sqdn	Germ.	Undercarriage retracted too soon during take off
745	04.06.56	F8	WK752	RAF FC	UK	Brakes failed on landing, ended in ditch
746	04.06.56	F8	WL138	19 Sqdn	UK	Lost power on approach, belly landed
747	18.06.56	F8	WF713	600 Sqdn	Malta	Undershot landing, undercarriage collapsed
748	28.06.56	F8	Wh355	FWS	UK	*Lost control in cloud, dived into ground*
749	28.06.56	T7	WL407	SF Wahn	Germ.	Canopy opened, baled out
750	30.06.56	F8	WB105	604 Sqdn	UK	Hit slipstream, wing hit ground, overshot, baled out
751	26.07.56	F8	WH421	611 Sqdn	Malta	Ran off runway on landing, hit wall
752	01.08.56	PR 10	WB180	13 Sqdn	Cyprus	Abandoned take off, hit by WB172
753	18.08.56	PR9	WB125	208 Sqdn	Malta	Throttle jammed on take off, ran off runway, caught fire
754	23.08.56	F8	WH374	63	UK	Belly landed accidentally, caught

			Sqdn			fire
755	26.08.56	F8	WE853	615 S	UK	*Hit by WH280, crashed*
756	26.08.56	F8	WH280	615Sq	UK	*Hit WE853, crashed*
757	27.08.56	F8	WK985	608 Sqdn	Moro.	*Both engines cut, baled out unsuccessfully*
758	11.09.56	F8	WK787	CF Turn.	UK	*High speed stall recovering from loop, crashed*
759	04.10.56	F8	WK874	247 Sqdn	UK	Undercarriage accidentally retracted after landing
760	05.10.56	F8	WL137	19 Sqdn	UK	*Lost control in cloud, dived into ground*
761	09.10.56	F8	WK801	65 Sqdn	UK	Hit slipstream causing hard landing, undercarriage collapsed
762	13.10.56	F8	WA855	41 Sqdn	UK	*Baled out unsuccessfully (reason unknown)*
763	30.11.56	PR 10	VS982	541 Sqdn	Germ	Abandoned take off, ran off runway
764	06.12.56	NF 13	WM314	39 Sqdn	Cyprus	*Crashed on night approach in bad weather (2)*
765	21.12.56	T7	WF848	FECS	Indon	*Lost control in cloud, dived into ground*

39 write-offs and 19 deaths in 1956

766	03.01.57	F8	WA879	74 Sqdn	UK	*Collided with WG974, baled out unsuccessfully*
767	03.01.57	F8	WG974	74 Sqdn	UK	*Collided with WA879, baled out unsuccessfully*
768	04.01.57	F8	WK681	65 Sqdn	UK	*Hit tree during low level exercise*
769	08.01.57	T7	WL479	RAFFC	UK	Lost other engine on single-engine approach, crash landed
770	14.01.57	F8	WE887	233 OCU	UK	*Collided with WH459, baled out unsuccessfully*
771	04.02.57	NF 14	WS753	25 Sqdn	UK	*Flew into high ground at night (2)*
772	25.02.57	FR9	VZ577	208 Sqdn	Iraq	Ran out of fuel, belly landed in desert
773	25.02.57	FR9	WB138	208 Sqdn	Iraq	Ran out of fuel, belly landed in desert
774	25.02.57	FR9	WX976	208	Iraq	Ran out of fuel, belly landed in

				Sqdn		desert
775	01.03.57	NF 13	WM31 0	39 Sqdn	Cyprus	Ran off end of runway

The 20 Squadrons of the Royal Auxiliary Air Force were disbanded on the 10th March 1957, and this was the end of my 8 year service in the UK Air Force. From 1947 to 1957 the Royal Auxiliary Air Force Squadrons had provided one third of the fighter strength of the United Kingdom, having the particular role of home defence.

776	24.03.57	FR9	VW370	208 Sqdn	Aden	*Engine fire, baled out unsuccessfully (at low altitude)*
777	28.03.57	F8	WH452	APS Sylt	Germ.	Undercarriage retracted accidentally while taxying
778	05.04.57	T7	VW432	208 Sqdn	Malta	*Lost power and lost control in landing circuit, crashed*
779	12.04.57	T7	WL410	FWS	UK	*Crashed during single engine practice in circuit (2)*
780	15.04.57	NF 11	WD725	29 Sqdn	UK	Abandoned take off, ran off runway, caught fire
781	17.04.57	F8	WL177	65 Sqdn	UK	Undercarriage collapsed on landing
782	03.06.57	T7	VW444	BF Sel.	Sing.	Swung off runway when tyre burst on take off
783	14.06.57	F8	WK981	FCCS	UK	Stalled on approach and hit radar dish
784	27.06.57	T7	WG961	SF Odi.	UK	*Stalled on single-engine approach, crashed*
785	26.07.57	F8	WK916	173 Sqdn	UK	Undershot landing, undercarriage torn off
786	08.08.57	T7	VW488	13 Gp	UK	*Crashed after take off in bad weather (2)*
787	20.08.57	F8	WK953	208 Sqdn	Malta	Hood opened on take off, ran off runway
788	27.09.57	FR9	WL261	208 Sqdn	Libya	Undercarriage leg jammed up, landed on 2 wheels
789	01.10.57	F8	WH250	APS Sylt	Germ.	Tyre blew on take off, fuselage damaged
790	11.10.57	F8	WA794	5 CAA	UK	*Flew into ground in bad visibility*

791	11.10.57	F8	WH346	APS Sylt	Germ .	Undercarriage leg jammed up, landed on 2 wheels
792	18.10.57	T7	WL368	CFE CF	UK	*Lost control in bad visibility, flew into ground (2)*
793	20.11.57	NF 14	WS830	64 Sqdn	UK	Lost control on approach at night, baled out
794	21.11.57	T7	WH204	83 Gp	Germ .	*Stalled on single-engine approach, crashed*
795	25.11.57	NF 12	WS638	72 Sqdn	UK	Hit by an F-84F, baled out

30 write-offs and 17 deaths in 1957

795 Meteors were written off, and over 400 pilots killed by accident in the Royal Air Force and Royal Auxiliary Air Force from the end of WWII in 1945 to the end of 1957. During my own time in the Air Force there were 680 Meteors written off causing 376 deaths, 329 of these deaths occurring while I was flying Meteors.

It is interesting to compare these accidental losses to the number of Meteors shot down in the 3 year Korean war from 1950 to 1953. By the end of the conflict, the Australian Meteor squadron had flown 4,836 missions, destroying six MiG-15s, over 3,500 structures and some 1,500 vehicles. 30 Meteors were lost due to enemy action.

On the other hand the peace time accidents described here do not compare with the 5,500 aircraft lost as described by Norman L. R. Franks in his 3 volumes of "RAF Fighter Command Losses of the Second World War" published by Midland, 2008, 1998, 2000 respectively.

(Hence the quote "Nothing to worry about"?)

APPENDIX 3 - ABBREVIATIONS

A&AEE	Aeroplane & Armament Exp. Est.	CGS	Central Gunnery School
AFDS	Air Fighting Development Squadron	CU	Conversion Unit
AFS	Advanced Flying School	DFLS	Day Fighter Leaders School
AH	Artificial Horizon	EFS	Empire Flying School
APC	Armament Practice Camp	ETPS	Empire Test Pilots School
AWOCU	All Weather Operational Conversion Unit	FCCS	Fighter Command Communications Sqdn
AWDS	All Weather Development Squadron	FECS	Far East Communications Flight
Belgm.	Belgium	FIDS	Fighter Interception Development Sqdn
BofB	Battle of Britain	FP	Ferry Pool
BF Sel.	Base Flight Selatar (Singapore)	FTU	Ferry Training Unit
CAACU	Civil Anti-Aircraft Cooperation Group	FWS	Fighter Weapons School
CBE	Central Bomber Establishment	Germ.	Germany
CF	Communications Flight	Gibr.	Gibraltar
CF Turn.	Communications Flight Turnhouse	Gp	Group
CFE	Central Fighter Establishment	I of AM	Institute of Aviation Medicine
CFS	Central Flying School	Indon.	Indonesia
ITF Nic.	Instrument Training Flight, Nicosia	PRDU	Photographic Reconnaissance Dev. Unit
Malay.	Malaya	RAE	Royal Aircraft Establishment
Medit.	Mediterranean	RAFFC	Royal Air Force Flying College

Met. Sect.	Metropolitan Sector	RRE	Radar Research Establishment
Moro.	Morocco	SF Bens.	Station Flight Benson
MU	Maintenance Unit	SF Brug.	Station Flight Bruggen
N11	NF11	SF Dux.	Station Flight Duxford
Neth.	Netherlands	SF Leuch.	Station Flight Leuchars
Norw.	Norway	SF Odi.	Station Flight Odiham
N.Sea	North Sea	SF Tang.	Station Flight Tangmere
Nth.Sect.	North Sector	Sing.	Singapore
OCU	Operational Conversion Unit	Sqdn, S, Sq, Sqd	Squadron
OFU	Overseas Ferry Unit	TFU	Telecommunications Flying Unit
P10	PR10	WEE	Winterisation Experimental Est.
P.Gulf	Persian Gulf		

References

1. James J. Halley M.B.E. "Broken Wings" Air Britain (Historians) Limited 1999

2. Derek N. James "Gloster Aircraft since 1917" Putnam 1987

3. Squadron/Signal Publication "Meteor in Action" by Glenn Ashley 1995

4. Gloster Meteor Mark 7 Pilot's Flight Operating Instructions, Periscope Film 2008 and Pilots Notes for Meteor 8 1955

5. Particular web site references (many others used) … The History of Royal Air Force Wittering *http://www.raf.mod.uk/rafwittering/aboutus/history.cfm*

   … The History of Royal Air Force Cottesmore *http://www.raf.mod.uk/rafcottesmore/aboutus/history.cfm*

   … The History of 616 South Yorkshire Squadron, Royal Auxiliary Air Force *http://www.raf.mod.uk/history/616squadron.cfm*

   … The History of 501 County of Gloucester Squadron, Royal Auxiliary Air Force *http://www.raf.mod.uk/history_old/h501.html*

   … Contribution to a Flight Global Forum "Missiles and Meteors" by B.R.A.Burns *http://www.flightglobal.com/pdfarchive/view/1989/1989%20-%200502.html* – *reproduced here:*

SIR—Without taking sides on the Tomcat v Flogger episode *(Flight,* January 14), photographic evidence of missiles carried on a fighter does not prove that it was acting aggressively. I believe that NATO air forces generally train with missiles equipped with active sensors, but without warheads.

Regarding the "Phantom Dive" diagnosis of the Meteor 7 accident at Coventry, reported in the same issue, it is tragic that the standard "crew room warning" of the 1950s was not passed on to the pilot concerned. The Meteor 7, with its deeper nose than the fighter variants, was directionally unstable with airbrakes out and undercarriage down. Service pilots of that era, flying as passengers or instructors in Meteor 7s, learned to keep their left hand by the airbrake lever, ready to push or hold it forward as the pilot selected undercarriage down.

B. R. A. BURNS

Ivy Dene Farm

Moorside

Treales

Preston PR4 3XH

Final Note: Any errors in the tables reproduced here will be my fault, not Mr. Halley's

Printed in Great Britain
by Amazon

21496132R00078